S0-EDP-370

Mel Bay Presents BUILDING

HARMONICA TECHNIQUE

By David Barrett

A Comprehensive Study of Harmonica Techniques and Blues Soloing Concepts
~For the Intermediate to Advanced Diatonic Harmonica Player~

CD CONTENTS

Visit us on the Web at http://www.melbay.com — E-mail us at email@melbay.com

David Barrett, Author

~Table Of Contents~

Harmonica Techniques

Section 1

Chapter 5 ~ Tongue Blocking

Chapter 6 ~ Acoustic Playing

Chapter 7 ~ Amplified Playing

~Theory & Application~
Section 2

Chapter 8 ~ Blues Scales

Chapter 9 ~ Octave Substitution

Chapter 10 ~ Playing Positions

Chapter 11 ~ Position Substitution

Soloing Techniques
Section 3

Chapter 12 ~ Lead

Chapter 13 ~ Accompaniment

Chapter 14 ~ Applying What You've Learned

Glossary Of Terms

Up Front

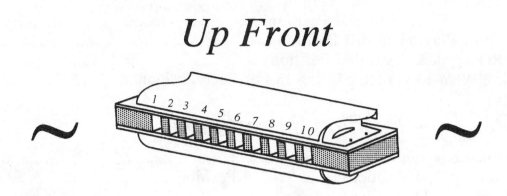

This book is an in-depth study of the harmonica designed to hone your harmonica playing skills and the musical thought needed to become a great player. My specialty is blues and this material will reflect that. I believe that blues harmonica is the most disciplined of all styles played on the harmonica, and in my opinion, if you can play blues you can play any style. The section "Harmonica Techniques" is designed to be non stylistic. As an instructor I feel it is my job to show any and every technique that is pertinent on the harmonica, and whether or not it fits your style is up to you. Some of the techniques I teach in this section will actually go beyond normal usage. You are the future of harmonica, and as every generation surpasses its predecessor, so will you surpass the players of today. Under the section "Theory & Application" I have compiled material based around the blues scales. I personally believe that an understanding of the blues scales, as applied to the harmonica, is the key to soloing and an understanding of all the playing positions. The third and last section "Soloing Techniques" is packed with exercises focused on helping you develop your soloing skills. As a harmonica player, every time you're asked to play, you're put into a soloing situation. This section, having been designed with that thought in mind, will carry you through the techniques which are used by the modern soloist. This book is not designed as a progressive lesson book. Though there are playable examples, it is up to you to develop the techniques taught in each section. To get the most out of this book you should play all the examples and try to develop some of the techniques on your own.

~Notation~

As a harmonica player you already have a couple things going for you. The harmonica by itself is unable to play in a wide key range. The original purpose of the diatonic harmonica was to have a separate harmonica for each key. Because of this, as a harmonica player you don't need to learn all the different keys and modes. What this means to you is that a riff on the C harmonica can be played on the F harmonica and the riff's positioning remains the same. The next thing going for you as a harmonica player is the notation used. Your harmonica is numbered one to ten, one being lowest and ten being highest. Standard notation uses five lines that make up a staff, how far up or down the staff the note is placed indicates the pitch of the note. Below this note on the staff are the numbers that correspond to the holes on your harmonica. Since each hole on your harmonica has its own separate pitch, you don't have to read music up and down the staff. So far we have almost completely negated all the reasons for using notated music, except one . . . rhythm. The only way for a writer to have complete control of the interpretation of his or her music is by a standard notational system that all musicians can understand. As you and I study together this written music is going to be our visual mode of learning. All the examples shown in this book are also accompanied by the tape, this is our aural mode of learning. Even if you're not proficient at reading notated rhythms, because of the tape, you will get just as much out of the book as someone who is. Many people are visually oriented so the notated music is for them. For people who read music, every example is written around the C harmonica pitch set, even if it is not played on a C harmonica. I have chosen to do this to aid people that aren't as good at reading music, and outside of harmonica study books there is no forum for harmonica players that read music. What I'm trying to get at is what there is written for the harmonica is written in tablature, and reading music that wasn't originally meant for the harmonica usually doesn't sit well with the note spread. Each examples' key signature will reflect the position it is played in. 1st position will have the key signature of C, 2nd position will have G, and 3rd position will have D. As you will read in this book, you'll see that harmonica players play on both the minor and major side, with blues being more on the minor side. Notationally I have chosen to write all the key signatures in major, the reason behind this being one: accompaniment is in major more than it is in minor, and two: bends and lowered scale degrees are visually more apparent when reading the notated music.

~Harmonica Notation~

When a hole number stands by itself below a note, it is to be drawn (3). When a hole number is followed by a plus, it is to be blown (3+). Below are some examples of the notation that you'll run into that are either not apparent at first glance or are specific to harmonica notation.

DOTTED VALUES

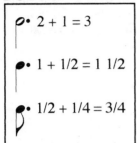

Dotted Values: A dot, notated to the right of a note head, extends its value by half. **ex**: A half note normally receives 2 beats; a dotted half receives 3 beats (2 + 1 = 3). A quarter note normally receives 1 beat; a dotted quarter receives 1 1/2 beats (1 + 1/2 = 1 1/2). An eighth note normally receives a 1/2 beat; a dotted eighth receives 3/4 of a beat (1/2 + 1/4 = 3/4).

TIE & SLUR

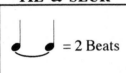

Tie & Slur: It is possible to combine the duration of successive notes of the <u>same pitch</u> using a curved line known as a **tie**. If the curved line connects successive notes of <u>different pitch</u>, it is called a **slur**. When a slur is used over a bend it means for you to play it smooth, not detached.

ACCENTS

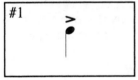

Accent #1: This accent means that the initial attack of the note is to have more body and volume. When performing this accent, don't just think loud and strong, but attack the note then taper down the volume and intensity.

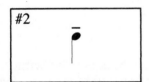

Accent #2: This accent means to give the note its utmost full length, and then more. This marking is often used in blues on the strong beat to give importance over the weak beat.

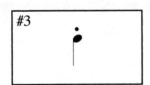

Accent #3: This accent is called a staccato. When you perform a note staccato you are to give the note a quick attack, then stop, thus giving the note a short duration. This marking is often used in blues on the weak beat to give importance to the strong.

SWING EIGHTHS

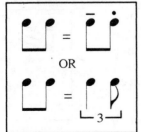

When playing blues, the triplet rhythmic feel dominates. When the marking to the left is given, it means to give the eighth note on the beat a longer duration, and to play the eighth note off the beat a slight bit later in time and shorter. This takes an otherwise very square and strict rhythm and gives it a rounder, more fluid feeling. <u>You will not usually see this marking in this book. All the music you will read in this book has this rhythmic feeling assumed, without it, it wouldn't sound like blues!</u>

~Specific Harmonica Notation~

DIP BEND

Dip Bend: The dip bend is produced by hitting a note that would normally be played straight with a slight bend, then raising it very quickly to its natural state. The dip bend is notated with a carrot like marking above the note. The dip bend is usually used when a bend is played to quick to be notated with a rhythmic value.

TONGUE BLOCK

Tongue Block: When a single hole is to be played with a tongue block embouchure, a small circle will be notated above the note head. As you will read in the chapter on tongue blocking the single hole tongue block is used along with a tongue slap to add thickness; I recommend using the tongue slap every time this marking is present.

TWO HOLE SHAKE

Two Hole Shake: The two hole shake, shown in chapter 4, is achieved by shaking your head between the two holes indicated below the two notes. The marking for the two hole shake is three slashes below the two note heads.

OCTAVE

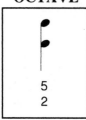

Octave: The octave embouchure, shown in chapter 5, is notated with the hole numbers you are supposed to play on the left and right side of your embouchure. The bottom number is the left side of your embouchure and the top number is the right side of your embouchure.

FLUTTER TONGUE

Flutter Tongue: The flutter tongue, shown in chapter 5, is notated in the same fashion as the octave is, but there are three slashes notated between the two note heads to tell you to do a flutter tongue. At first glance it's easy to mistake this marking for a two hole shake, but remember that the two hole shake has the three slashes below both note heads not between.

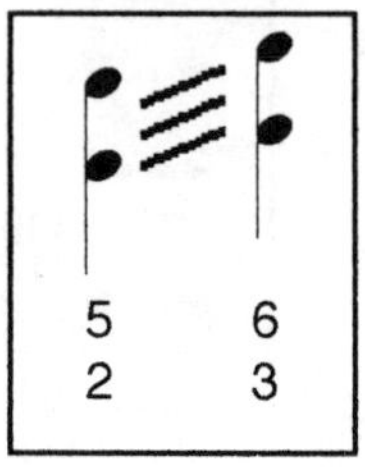

Octave Shake: The octave shake, shown in chapter 5, is notated with three slashes between the two octaves that you are to shake between.

OCTAVE SHAKE

5 6
2 3

Bending

When soloing on the harmonica, I'm constantly thinking of three things, what's my next lick, where's it going to take me, and how I'm going to pour all of my emotions into this one solo. The first two are usually accomplished by knowing my favorite licks so well that I can rewrite them as I play to accommodate each particular song. How I accomplish the third is by playing the soulful bends that the harmonica, with a little coaxing, is very willing to give me.

Bends add that extra dimension of expression that every blues player, from a guitarist to a saxophonist, uses to pull every possible emotion out of his or her instrument. At first, bending will feel a little awkward. When you rode a bike for the first time, I bet that also felt a little awkward. Riding a bike is a technique that takes balance, agility, and control. After riding for a while those techniques became a part of you. To make a right turn you no longer had to think to turn the handle bar, reduce your speed, and lean into the turn. Those techniques of riding a bike are now embedded in you. Your brain now thinks instantaneously in conjunction with the controlled response of your body. Playing bends on the harmonica hold to those same principles. By working slowly and mastering each exercise, when it comes time to learn new licks and solos, you'll know exactly what to do for your bends because you've already played them. Bending can be very frustrating at times, but be patient and persevere, the exercises to come are there to help you become that master harmonica player.

What Is A Bend?

The actual act of bending is achieved by the positioning of your tongue in relation to your mouth. Your embouchure needs to be in such a position that it creates an air cavity between your tongue and the roof of your mouth. This small air cavity takes an otherwise large and relaxed air passage, that creates a warm and soft air stream, and constricts it into a passage of smaller diameter, that creates a cold and fast air stream. The whole purpose of doing this is to make an air stream through your harmonica that actually bends the draw reed inward and the blow reed outward, thus making a lowered pitch.

What Happens To My Harmonica When I Bend?

When you blow in a hole on your harmonica, the force of your air stream vibrates a reed on the blow reed plate. When you draw in a hole on your harmonica, the force of your air stream vibrates a reed on the draw reed plate. When bending on the harmonica, the actual draw reed bends inward and transfers the vibrations to the blow reed. To check out this phenomenon for yourself take off the cover plates from one of your old battered harmonicas and go to a mirror and bend the 4 draw. Notice that as you bend, the reed actually pulls inward and little by little the 4 blow reed starts to vibrate. Now put your fingertip and press down on the 4 draw reed and you'll hear that the bend is still sounding. If you've ever wondered why your four blow is often the first reed to go flat, this might give you an idea how much stress your 4 blow goes through.

Draw Bend: Upper Reed Vibrates

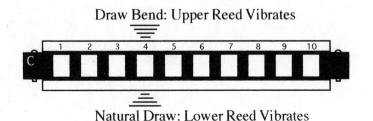

Natural Draw: Lower Reed Vibrates

Bends Available On Your Harmonica

To start off, let's look at what notes the harmonica is willing to give us during a bend. Written below is a look at the natural note selection for the diatonic harmonica.

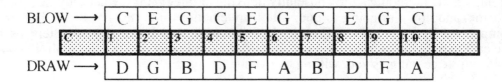

The notational system used to measure how far you can bend a note on the harmonica is that of half steps and whole steps. Let's look together at the piano to see where these half steps and whole steps land.

The Octave

The first step to understanding music is to look at the octave. The root of the octave can be at any given point on the piano. An octave happens when the next note up or down the piano with the same letter name is sounded.

Major Scale On The Piano

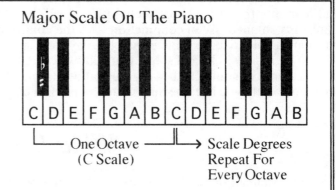

Half Steps & Whole Steps

In the major scale, there is a series of half steps and whole steps that it uses for its construction. A half step happens where two white keys lay side by side (A), or when a white key is followed by a black key, and vise versa (B). A whole step happens where two keys are separated by one key (C).

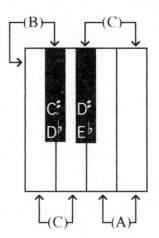

Order Of Half Steps & Whole Steps

Most music uses this major scale for its construction. This scale, as shown above, has a set order of half steps and whole steps that gives it the sound it does.

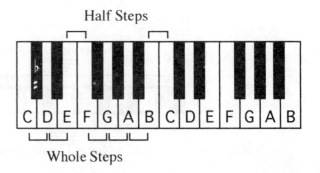

The Major Scale On Your Harmonica

The easiest way to understand these half steps and whole steps is to play and listen to them. Looking back at the harmonica diagram on page 10 notice that you can get a major scale starting on 4 blow and ending on 7 blow. Play the example below and listen very carefully to the half steps that happen between the 5 blow and 5 draw, and the 7 draw and 7 blow. Play through the scale a second time and play only up to the 7 draw, and then stop! Can you hear and feel the yearning of wanting to resolve by half step to the 7 blow? That is what half steps give us. It gives chords and melodies the pulling quality of needing to be resolved to some where else.

How These Half And Whole Steps Effect Your Bends

Since the blow reed is the actual reed that vibrates during the bend, <u>you can only bend down as far as a half step above the natural tone given on that blow reed</u>. To further understand this let's look at all the bendible notes on the draw side of the harmonica in relation to the blow side. Looking at the chart below notice that the distance between the 1 blow and 1 draw is a whole step (C to D). That only leaves us with a half step bend, the D-flat. The distance between the 2 blow and 2 draw is a step and one half (E to G). That leaves us with a whole step worth of bends (G-flat and F). The distance between the 3 blow and 3 draw is two whole steps (G to B). That leaves us with a step and one half worth of bends (B-flat to A-flat). Looking at the distance between the 4 blow and 4 draw notice that it's the same as hole number 1, so the same half step bend applies. The distance between the 6 blow and 6 draw is a whole step (G to A). That leaves us with a half step bend, the A-flat.

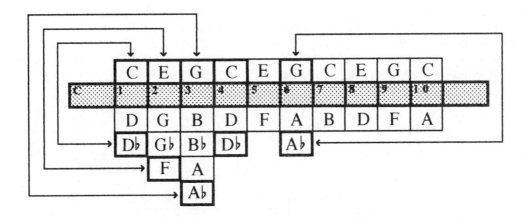

Looking at the 5 draw and 7 draw notice that they are the natural half steps that land within the major scale. Since the half step is the smallest amount of distance between two notes, there is no bend possible for these two holes. After you learn how to bend you'll notice that you can get a slight bend out of the 5 draw. Since this bend cannot be used in a diatonic context, mostly a bend on the 5 draw is used for feeling and expression. What I want to do now is classify these two different types of bends. The first classification is a melodic bend, and the second classification is a stylistic bend. A melodic bend happens when the tune asks for a specific bend. A stylistic bend is a decoration of the tune, and the bend can be taken at any degree without changing the contour of the tune. Refer to measure 9 of Big Boy's Jam on page 68 for an example of how a stylistic 5 draw bend can be used.

High End Blow Bends

When playing the major scale on the previous page the pattern was blow, draw, blow, draw, and then right after the 6 draw the harmonica did a back flip. On the 7th hole and above, the harmonica changes to having the blow higher than the draw. Since the blow reed is higher than the draw, the draw bend has no blow reed to bend down to and interact with for a half step bend. This means that there are no bends available to us on the draw side of the high end of our harmonica, but there are blow bends available. Looking at the 7 blow and 7 draw, there is no half step in between them, so there is no bend possible. The 8 blow and 8 draw are separated by a half step, so the half step bend E-flat is available. The 9 blow and 9 draw are separated by a half step, so the half step bend G-flat is available. The 10 blow and 10 draw are separated by a whole step, so the half step bend B is available, and the whole step bend B-flat is available.

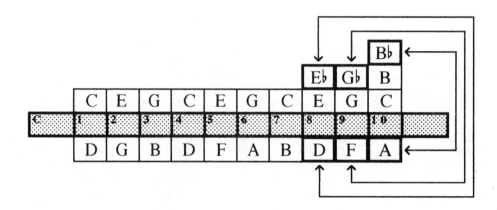

Bending Notation

The notation for bending will use a slash for each half step you are to bend. On three draw you are able to bend three half steps. For a half step bend on the 3 draw you'll see a three with one slash (3'). For a whole step bend on the 3 draw you'll see a three with two slashes (3"). For a step and one half bend on the 3 draw you'll see a three with three slashes (3'''). The chart below illustrates all the bends possible on the harmonica with their corresponding bend symbols.

Bend Chart

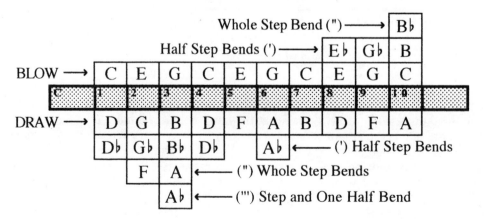

Getting Started

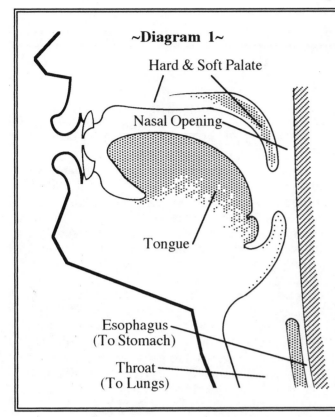

~Diagram 1~

Hard & Soft Palate

Nasal Opening

Tongue

Esophagus (To Stomach)

Throat (To Lungs)

Before we can go into the actual act of bending, we need to consider how the different parts of your mouth interact with each other. Diagram 1 shows a side view of your mouth. At the roof of your mouth is the hard palate and soft palate. The hard palate, even though it doesn't move, is the second most important part in your bending. When you drive a car you need two elements: the car, and the hard pavement you drive upon. The hard palate is just like that pavement. Just as pavement gives a car a surface to maneuver upon, the hard palate gives your tongue a surface to maneuver upon.

Learning Tip

As you read through the next couple of pages, take a mental picture of all of the bending diagrams. Remember them well so you can work on your bends when you don't have this book at hand. To this day I still work on bending techniques to improve my playing. In my opinion clean, articulate, and well thought out bends are the trademarks of a good harmonica player.

Step One In Your Bending

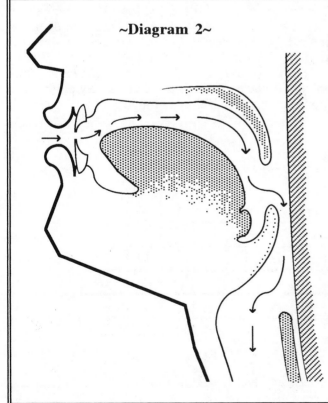

~Diagram 2~

When blowing or drawing, your tongue should be in a natural relaxed position like in diagram 2. By having your tongue in this relaxed position it allows your air stream to flow freely from your harmonica, through your mouth and down to your lungs. Remember not to allow air to leak through your nose. This will produce a whiny tone and you'll run out of breath quickly, especially during bending. Look at diagram 1 again at the nasal opening. This opening is the pathway to your entire nasal system. To stop the leakage through your nose, think as if you have a cold and you're trying to stop that annoying stream of phlegm from flowing down your throat. You'll find that the air passage that links your nose to your mouth has a controllable muscle. By tightening that muscle you can stop the air leakage and you'll find that you can play longer, cleaner, and stronger than before. If you're not sure you're leaking air through your nose, after learning how to bend, plug your nose with your fingers. If you were leaking air before, you'll feel and hear a large difference in your bend.

Step Two In Your Bending

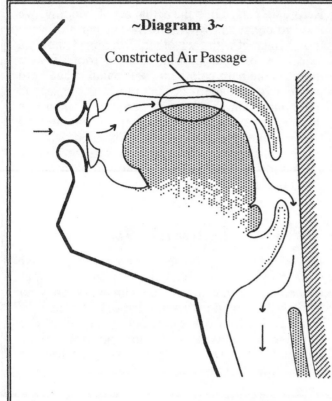

~Diagram 3~

Constricted Air Passage

Diagram 3 shows what your tongue should look like in the bent position. Notice that the air passage is constricted between your tongue and the back of the roof of your mouth. When first trying to bend say the syllables **E - O** in your deepest voice possible without the harmonica. When pronouncing the **E**, the front of your tongue is in the natural position and the back of your tongue is touching the bottom of your upper molars. Pronouncing the letter **E** is what gets your tongue in the right position to bend. When pronouncing the **O**, your jaw drops and your tongue is forced to the back of your mouth creating a constricted air passage. Center your lips on the 4 draw and make sure that you're only sounding the 4 draw throughout your bend. If you catch just a little bit of a neighboring hole while trying to bend, it's enough to stop you from making a full bend. As you draw into the fourth hole say the syllables **E - O**. Remember to think tight and not to let any air leak through the sides of your tongue. You want to get your full air stream through the constricted air cavity and by doing so you should be able to feel the cold air stream through the top center of your mouth.

Extra Help

If you were able to bend right after you read that, you are truly one of the gifted few. Some people get lucky and find the right positioning in their mouth right away and are able to bend. For most people it takes a good week or so of experimenting. Keep trying! If the syllables E - O don't work for you, try the word **BOY**. Say **BOY** a couple of times before picking up your harmonica to get used to the positioning of your tongue. Now take the **B** off to get the syllable **OY**. If you can only hear a slight bend, think tighter and more rigid in your embouchure. If you can't tell if you're getting a bend or not, try playing the corresponding bent note on a piano or guitar using your bend chart. Below is the bend chart to remind you what bends on the harmonica are available to you.

Bend Chart

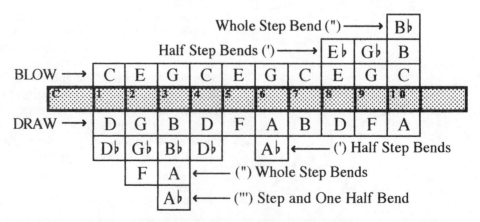

								Whole Step Bend (") →	B♭
							Half Step Bends (') →	E♭	G♭	B
BLOW →	C	E	G	C	E	G	C	E	G	C
	0	1	2	3	4	5	6	7	8	9	10
DRAW →	D	G	B	D	F	A	B	D	F	A
	D♭	G♭	B♭	D♭		A♭	← (') Half Step Bends
	F	A	← (") Whole Step Bends
	A♭	← (''') Step and One Half Bend

Step Three In Your Bending

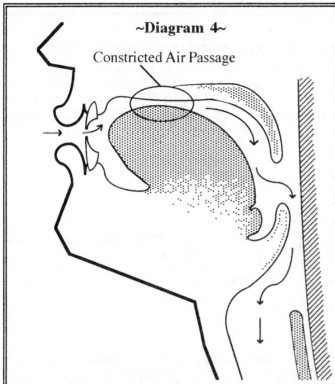

~Diagram 4~

Constricted Air Passage

When bending on the 6 draw, your tongue is in a different position than if you were bending the 2 draw. As you go up on the harmonica bending, your tongue needs to be more in the front of your mouth. Diagram 4 shows how much farther your tongue needs to be for the higher bends. Instead of using E-O, or OY, lets use **SHHH**. Try saying **SHHH** a couple of times and feel how much farther to the front of your mouth your tongue is. Now try it with your harmonica on the 6 draw. If you start to get the bend and then it disappears, you're actually going past the bend. Try the same bend but work your tongue slower from the natural position to the bent position and stop right before the bend wants to stop sounding.

Blow Bends

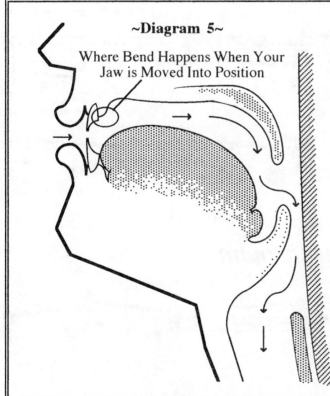

~Diagram 5~

Where Bend Happens When Your Jaw is Moved Into Position

The first thing that needs to be considered about blow bends is what key of harmonica you're using. When doing blow bends the key of harmonica should be a C or below, anything above a C the reeds are to short and stiff to bend. Looking at diagram 5, notice how far your tongue is in the front of your mouth in relation to the other bending embouchures. Since the reeds are so short and stiff on the high end, it takes a strong rigid embouchure to get a bend. For a blow bend, the tip of your tongue should curl behind the front part of your bottom set of teeth. While performing a blow bend your tongue stays stiff and rigid, your jaw is what moves up and down to create the bend. By doing this you have complete strength and control for the bend. When you first try a blow bend, put your tongue in position behind your teeth and with a high amount of pressure hiss like a snake through the hole. Don't worry about blowing to hard, the high end bends need a lot of pressure to happen.

Bending Exercises

The bending examples to come are there to help at each stage of your progressing talent. One thing you must keep in mind when reading through these exercises is that they can't be rushed through. If you're a beginning player, it might take you a good year to be able to play through these exercises well. Like stated before, this book is not meant for the absolute beginner, so I have to accommodate the advanced players. None of the exercises, except for the ones shown on page 18, will have slur markings. Since these are bending exercises they should be practiced both slurred and detached.

Stopping At The Bottom

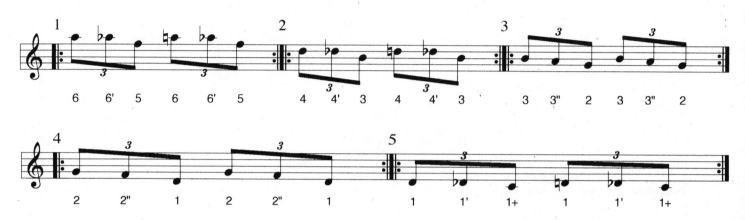

Going Up

Bent Turnaround

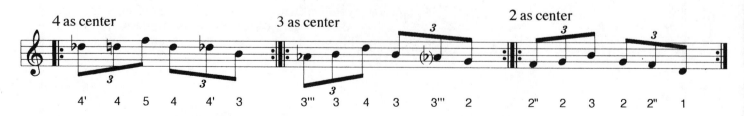

The bent turnaround, at bottom of the previous page, is one of my favorite bending exercises. This exercise develops your bends in two ways. First: It helps you get used to starting in the bent position and then having to go straight to an unbent note. Second: This exercise helps you develop the skill it takes to make smooth transitions between the lower notes. Use this exercise with the 4 draw as your center, 3 draw as your center, and 2 draw as center. When you're able to do this exercise comfortably try some of your licks that use the bottom end bends and I bet they'll sound smoother and you can play them with more ease. The bent shakes, shown below, will take you a good deal of time to play them smoothly. Make a mental note to yourself to make sure that every bent note is fully bent. When doing the exercises below, it's common for the bend to slowly lose its strength when it's taken faster. Take all the exercises slow and then speed up when you're confident that you're playing them perfect at the slow speed.

Bent Shakes

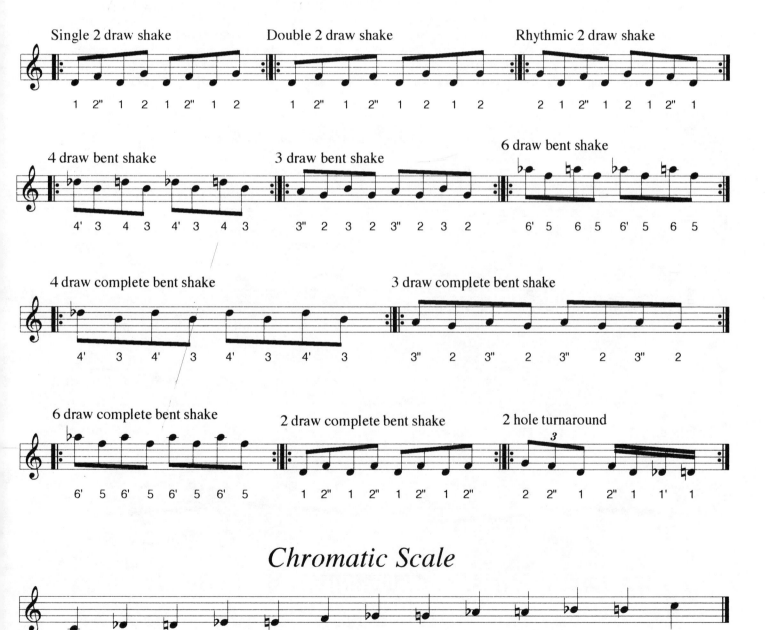

Chromatic Scale

After your bends have developed, you'll find that there are an awful lot of bends available to you on the bottom end. In fact you can almost get a complete chromatic scale starting on the 1 blow and ending on the 4 blow. The chromatic scale is a scale that starts on a given note and hits all the half steps all the way until the octave. The only note that is not available to us on our chromatic scale is the E-flat. As we study the blues scales later in this book this missing note plays a big role in our soloing. When going through the chromatic scale at the bottom of the previous page listen very carefully and try to match the pitch of the tape for every bend. If you have a piano at your disposal that's even better because you can control how fast you practice these bends. To do a chromatic scale on the piano start on middle C and hit every note, white and black keys, all the way up to the next C.

High End Blow Bends

Blow bends at first are actually fairly easy to do, but the tough part is to play them like you do the lower bends. When performing these exercises remember to use your jaw as the moving part of your bending embouchure. The blow bends are kind of like the 6 draw bend was when you first tried it. If you move your embouchure just a little bit out of phase you'll lose the bend, or go right past it. One thing that you may have found is that the 10 blow doesn't want to give you the half step bend, only the whole step bend. You're not alone, the 10 blow pretty much just snaps into the whole step bend and there isn't much you can do to control it. Don't worry if you're unable to do the half step bend, in all of my studies of the blues I've never heard the half step bend in a musical context.

Practicing Your Blow Bends

A Last Word About Developing Your Bends

In my opinion clean, articulate, and well thought out bends are a trademark of a good player. Challenge yourself to do your best on these exercises and don't settle for just good enough. After you feel competent on all the bending exercises, go back and play all the bends that are slurred detached. You'll find that it makes the exercises quite a bit more challenging.

Throat Vibratos

I believe some techniques on the harmonica are too important to pass by; and the throat vibrato is one of them. The vibrato is used to add warmth and expression to your playing. Without this throat vibrato, your playing will sound thin and lack emotion. The true test of a harmonica player's tone is to see how well they can solo to slow blues. Most harmonica players devote their time in developing speed, thus not giving their tone a chance to mature. The most effective technique you can use to enhance your tone is the throat vibrato. The throat vibrato takes off all the rough edges and gives your playing a more singing like quality, thus allowing you to sustain notes for longer periods of time in slow blues.

Where The Vibrato Happens

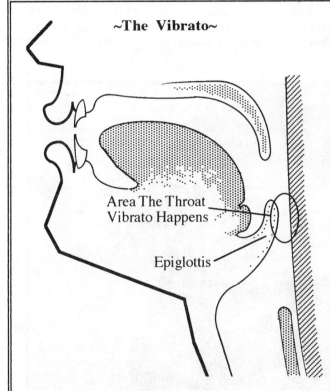

~The Vibrato~

Area The Throat Vibrato Happens

Epiglottis

When a singer or instrumentalist does a vibrato it is produced by rapid variations in pitch done very deep within their diaphragm. One thing you have to keep in mind is all instrumentalists and singers exhale to create music; a harmonica player can both inhale and exhale to create music. As blues or country musicians we spend most of our playing time inhaling, so harmonica players had to actually recreate the vibrato to accommodate this new playing style. There are three distinct vibratos that I find useful to the harmonica player, and each of these vibratos happen at different degrees of depth within your throat. The first two vibratos, that are discussed below, I believe are controlled where the epiglottis touches the back of your throat. By closing this area of your throat you can stop your air flow. When this part of your throat is closed off in a rhythmic fashion, you can create what I call the "laughing vibrato" and the "staccato vibrato."

The Laughing Vibrato

The laughing vibrato is a soft attack done with your throat that sounds just like a Santa Claus laugh. Before picking up your harmonica try saying **Ha Ha Ha Ha**. Notice that your air stream is constant and your throat blocks off the air stream in a rhythmic fashion. Now inhale saying the same syllables, but use more muscle in your throat to control the vibrato. This vibrato is relatively easy to get the hang of and most harmonica players use this vibrato.

The Staccato Vibrato

This vibrato was first introduced to me by professional blues harmonica player Gary Smith. The way he described this vibrato was like an inverted machine gun. Remember when you were a kid making machine gun noises with your throat to make it sound as if you were shooting someone; well this vibrato is just like that. Try the machine gun noise exhaling and then try inhaling to create the staccato vibrato.

The staccato vibrato isn't used much on the single hole, but is used often when drawing on two or more holes. At first, the staccato vibrato might feel weird because it feels like your choking, but after a while most people get used to it.

The Bent Vibrato

The bent vibrato is the most widely used by professional players because it has the same characteristics of a singer's vibrato. This vibrato sounds very sweet, and unlike the laughing vibrato and staccato vibrato, you are actually changing the pitch of the note up and down like the waver in a singer's voice. The bent vibrato happens deeper in the throat compared to the other two vibratos and gives you a thicker tone. By utilizing the deeper part of your throat you can create a slower vibration and actually bend the note downward to create a change in pitch. Remember back to the bending chapter when I stated that there had to be a constricted air passage to create a bend. When performing this vibrato you're choking off the air stream, and when doing so, you're making a constricted air passage creating a rhythmic bend with your throat. This vibrato can't really be explained thorough enough to give it justice, so listen carefully to the tape. When performing the bent vibrato your tongue has nothing to do with bending action, so if you feel your tongue moving, find the right position in your mouth for your tongue so it doesn't interfere. I feel the best way to develop your bent vibrato is to use the vibrato every time you're hanging on a note that's longer than a quarter note; your throat vibrato might sound choked and uneven now, but with time and practice, it will improve.

GARY SMITH

Gary Smith hails from the San Jose, San Francisco Bay Area of California. Being a mainstay in the west-coast blues scene for many years, Gary Smith has proven his capabilities in both song writing and on the harmonica, his primary instrument. If you ever have a chance to hear him, live or on recording, you'll hear many of the techniques taught in this book used to their fullest.

Photo By:
Leslie Ann Knight

Two Hole Shakes

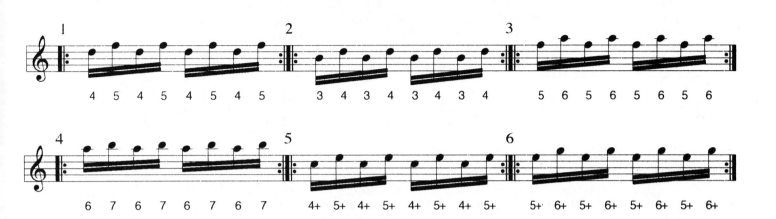

To perform a shake, hold your harmonica with both hands firmly and let your head make the shaking movement. Always start your shake with the bottom note; this gives the listener a sense of a melodic line on the bottom. The example below is meant for you to get used to shakes, and the transition between shakes. Notice that the quarter note sets you up for your next shake. The last example shows you how shakes will be presented on the staff. The notation for a shake is three slanted lines below both note heads with the two numbers written below you're to shake between.

Controlled Shakes

Shakes As Shown In Notation

Shakes Used As Variation

The two hole shake is used in two basic ways. The first is to use the two hole shake by itself, introducing the shake and ending the shake with a basic lick. The second way is to use the shake as a variation of a line used earlier in a solo. The shake itself is an ornamentation, the bottom note being the melodically important note and the top note being the decoration of the bottom note. The example written below is from the fourth 12 bar solo of Big Boy's Jam on page 69.

As you can see and hear, within the first four bars is the original lick. The fifth and sixth bar is the variation. Contrasting both licks you will see that the bottom notes remain the same. by doing the shake, you are adding an upper note, making a decoration of the lower. Within most of my soloing I use the shake as decoration just like the example above shows. Written below is what was just explained.

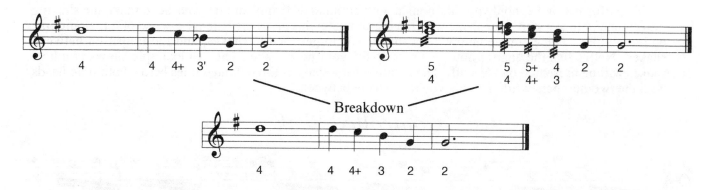

The example below is another exercise to help you get used to shakes. At first don't think of this as a song that's played all the way through; take it part by part. The second time around play it all the way through to help you develop breath control. The marking that indicates to take a breath is a small comma looking mark written above the staff.

More Shakes

Tongue Blocking

Tongue Blocking Embouchure

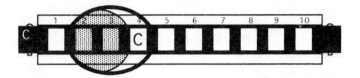

Tongue blocking is achieved by pursing your lips over three holes, blocking two holes to the left, and sounding the hole to the right. The three main reasons for using tongue blocking are shown below.

Tone (Attack): The original usage of tongue blocking was to create an embouchure to play single holes. Quickly this technique caught on as much more than that. When in the tongue blocking embouchure your lips are over three holes and two of those holes are blocked by your tongue. If you draw in first and then quickly slap your tongue into position all the air that it took to vibrate three holes is then punched through the one hole left over. The effect is a thicker sound because of the initial vibration of the three holes, and a wicked attack on the hole left over. This technique is often referred to as a <u>tongue slap</u> and is the most important reason for using tongue blocking.

Availability Of Octaves: Tongue blocking octaves is similar to straight tongue blocking in the way that you're still blocking two holes with your tongue, but instead of sounding just the hole to the right you're also sounding the hole to your left. If you're already playing with your tongue on the harmonica, to play an octave all you have to do is open your mouth a little wider. This allows for quick access to any octave that is available to you on that part of the harmonica.

Can Be Physically Faster and More Accurate: Say that I'm playing the 2 draw and I want to make a jump to the 6 blow, if I were to use a single hole embouchure, it would be quite a jump. If I were to go from playing a single hole 2 draw to a tongue blocked 6 blow I could get to the 6 blow physically faster and with a higher percentage of accuracy of hitting that note. This technique is a little more on the preference side, so try the technique and see if you can get better accuracy.

Octave Embouchure

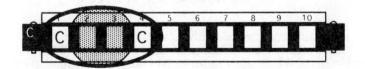

As stated before, tongue blocking octaves is similar to straight tongue blocking in the way that you're still blocking two holes with your tongue, but instead of sounding just the hole to the right, you're also sounding the hole to your left. Octaves are usually played to <u>thicken and enhance the sound of a given note on the harmonica</u>. When a harmonica player plays backup in a band, he or she will usually use octaves to thicken the tone of the harmonica and give it a broader sound like an organ. Looking at the note spread for the harmonica on the next page, notice that with a four hole tongue block embouchure you can get clean octaves all the way up the blow end of the harmonica. Tongue blocking octaves can also be used on the draw end of the harmonica, but you need to change your embouchure to accommodate the different note spread.

BLOW →	C	E	G	C	E	G	C	E	G	C
	1	2	3	4	5	6	7	8	9	10
DRAW →	D	G	B	D	F	A	B	D	F	A

4 Hole Draw Octaves

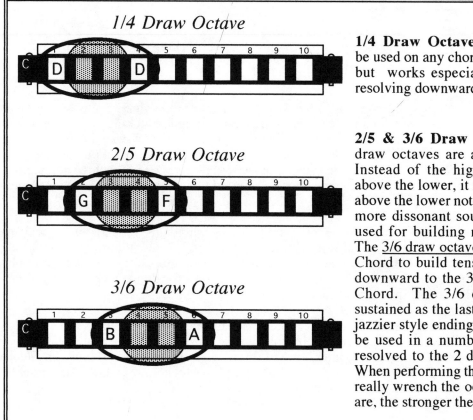

1/4 Draw Octave

2/5 Draw Octave

3/6 Draw Octave

1/4 Draw Octave: The 1/4 draw octave can be used on any chord of the blues progression, but works especially well on the V Chord resolving downward to the IV Chord.

2/5 & 3/6 Draw Octave: The 2/5 and 3/6 draw octaves are actually not true octaves. Instead of the higher note being an octave above the lower, it is actually a minor seventh above the lower note. This makes for a thicker more dissonant sounding octave that can be used for building musical tension in a solo. The 3/6 draw octave is usually used on the V Chord to build tension, and then is resolved downward to the 3/6 blow octave on the IV Chord. The 3/6 draw octave can also be sustained as the last note in a song to make a jazzier style ending. The 2/5 draw octave can be used in a number of ways, but is usually resolved to the 2 draw, 6 blow, or 4 draw. When performing the 2/5 and 3/6 draw octaves really wrench the octave, the louder the notes are, the stronger the dissonance.

Flutter Tongue

Flutter Tongue is performed by pulling your tongue on and off the blocked holes very quickly in a stabbing like motion while at all times sounding the octave. When performing the flutter tongue it has been traditionally used with the 4 hole draw octave. Technically it can also be used with the 5 hole draw octave, but musicians who use it are usually very advanced in their abilities. For most people the flutter tongue is hard to make the transition from sporatic to rhythmically even, but unlike vibratos this technique can be practiced and mastered in a fair amount of time. The flutter tongue is notated like the two hole shake is with the three slashes (A), but for flutter tongue the three slashes are notated between the two note heads of the octave that you are sounding (B).

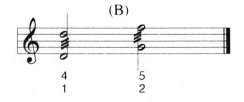

5 Hole Draw Octaves

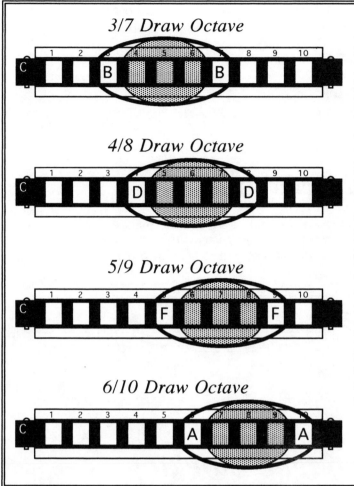

3/7 Draw Octave

4/8 Draw Octave

5/9 Draw Octave

6/10 Draw Octave

If you were to continue up the draw side of the harmonica keeping your embouchure the same you would get the same kind of dissonance that you did with the 2/5, 3/6 draw octaves. By switching your embouchure from tongue blocking two holes in the middle to blocking three holes you can get four more clean octaves up the draw side of your harmonica. These high end octaves are not used often, but when they are, you'll surely hear it. The high notes by themselves already stand out a great deal and by doubling the note making an octave they stand out even more. The human ear picks up high frequencies very well and even though the high end octaves on our harmonica are true octaves, if one of the notes in the octave is out of tune just a little bit, it sends a very dissonant message to the listener's ear. The whole idea of playing octaves on the low end of the harmonica is to send a broad message of <u>one thick note</u>. If your high end draw octaves are out of tune, they can't send that message, so be careful that the harmonica you're using is in tune

Octave Shake

Another technique used from octaves is the octave shake. The two hole shake on the lower to mid range of the harmonica is achieved by shaking your head between the two holes you wish to sound in a rhythmic fashion. The octave shake is the same in the respect that you shake between two holes, but the two holes are separated by a minor seventh for the 2/5 and 3/6 draw octaves, and an octave in all other cases.

Blow Octave Shake

Since the blow octaves are all pure octaves, any two hole shake on the blow side can be used as an octave shake. Below is an example of some of the substitutions that are used.

Draw Octave Shake

The 4 hole draw octave embouchure, since not a pure octave, isn't normally used for substitution but as a technique in itself. Below is an example of some of the draw octave shakes that are used.

5 Hole Draw Octave Shake

The 5 hole draw octave, being pure octaves, technically could be used in the place of any two hole draw shake above the 3 draw. As stated before, this technique isn't used often, but who knows, this might become your favorite technique. Below is an example of where the 5 hole draw octave shake can be used.

Where I Use Tongue Blocking

Tongue blocking in general is used in different ways by different artists; there are no set rules where it works best. Some people will use tongue blocking exclusively by just moving their tongue to the right and sounding the hole to the left for the lower end of the harmonica. I personally do not use tongue blocking below the fourth hole because of bends. I can get cleaner, faster, and more articulate bends from a single hole embouchure. As a studying harmonica player all I have to say is if you like the way the tongue blocking technique sounds, don't cut yourself short, learn it. If you are a more advanced player I challenge you to start substituting some of your licks that use a single hole embouchure to tongue blocking where pertinent. The examples below are exercises and songs you can use for tongue blocking. Take your time and play these slowly, tongue blocking, if not played cleanly will just make your playing sound sloppy instead of stronger.

Getting The Feel Of Tongue Blocking

For the exercise below play through it once using single holes, then use tongue blocking. After you have the feel of tongue blocking down try the tongue slap technique.

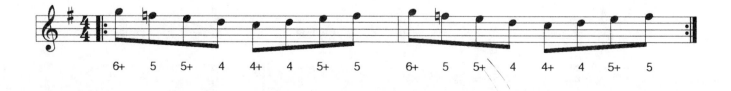

26

Octave Practice

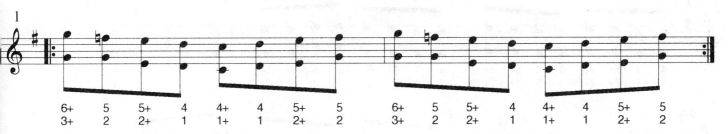

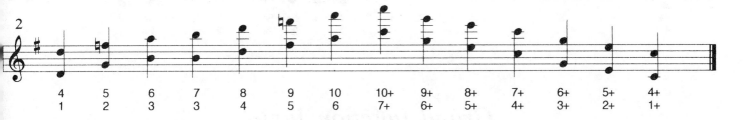

Embouchure Switch

Octave Boogie

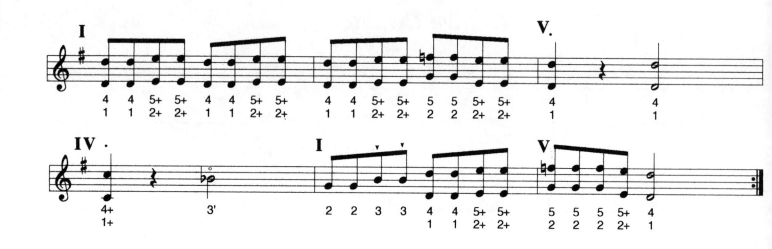

Grand Junction Jump

Acoustic Playing

When musicians say they're playing acoustically, all they're stating is that their instrument is not being altered in any electronic form by amplification. I feel that any time a harmonica player is holding something that doesn't allow them full usage of their hands they're amplified. If the harmonica player is holding nothing in their hands and are amplified by means of just a microphone in front of them, I consider that to be acoustic. By having a microphone in front of the player all that microphone is doing is amplifying what the listener's ear would naturally hear. As soon as you start changing how an instrument is heard, you not only change the tone color of the instrument but how the instrument is played. The best example of this would be the electric guitar. When the electric guitar was first introduced it completely changed the way the instrument was played even though it technically was still the same instrument. This new way of amplification made way for a tremendous amount of new styles because a band no longer had to have naturally loud instruments like horns, but could use smaller hard to hear instrument such as the harmonica. When harmonica players started using hand held microphones, like the bullet microphone, at that point the evolution of the harmonica started because it now had a medium in which it could be heard. Because of this new medium harmonica players were given new techniques to work with and subsequently left others to the wayside like hand techniques. After forty odd years of evolution the two styles have branched in their own directions and to the modern harmonica player the word acoustic isn't just a name but a stylistic way of playing. This section is going to cover some of the wonderful techniques involved in playing acoustically and will give you some common progressions used so you too can become an acoustic player.

Hand Techniques

The first aspect of hand techniques we're going to look at is the actual cupping of your hands on the harmonica. Pick one hand to be your primary holding hand, for right handed people it's usually their left hand. Picture A and A1 shows what your primary holding hand should look like while holding your harmonica. The other hand is going to be your cupping hand. Picture B and B1 shows what your cupping hand should look like in the cupped position. On both hands, all your fingers should be closed tightly together, this will make for an air tight cup.

(A) Holding Hand   (A1) Holding Hand

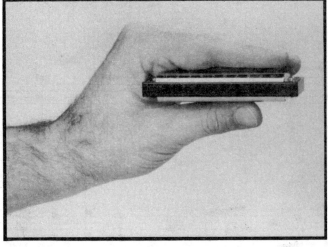
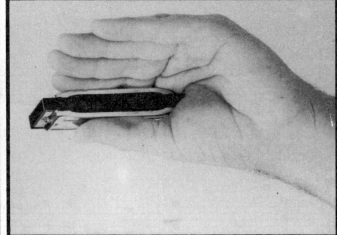

(B) Placement Of Finger On Cupping Hand

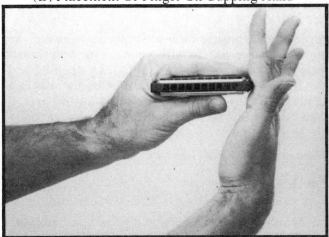

(B1) Cupping Hand

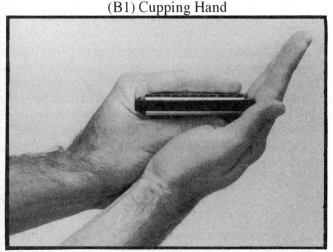

The most important aspect of your cup is when it is closed, it should be are tight. Cup your hands together around your harmonica and look to see if there are any openings where air could possibly escape. The main cupping techniques are spelled out below.

The WaWa

When your hands are closed, the tone it creates is soft and muffled. When your hands are open, it creates a contrast that is brighter and louder. If you were to sound a note on the harmonica and suddenly open your hands from the closed position, the tone variance would give you a WA effect. This technique is usually accompanied by a slight up-bend as you open your hands, thus giving an increased WA effect.

The Hand Vibrato

If you were to take your wawa effect and speed it up you would get a hand vibrato. There are two ways I create the hand vibrato, the first being opening my cup from the bottom, and the second opening my cup from the side. Opening the cup from the bottom is the slower of the two, but is easier to return to the cupped position. For the side vibrato put your hands up in a praying like position, and then tilt your hands to a comfortable position. After you have done this, shift your bottom hand around until it feels comfortable because that is the hand that is going to be doing all the movement. When doing the vibrato your bottom hand will move in a clapping like motion with both palms connected acting as a pivot. If the vibrato feels uncomfortable to do, try moving your hands a little more vertical and tilt your head more to accommodate. Pictures C and C1 show what your hands should look like when opening your cup from the bottom and side.

(C) Opening Your Cup From The Bottom

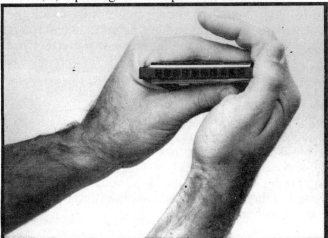

(C1) Opening Your Cup From The Side

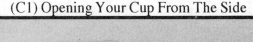

Rhythmic Hand Vibrato

The hand vibrato can be used fast or slow, it all depends on the presentation you're trying to make. In some instances the hand vibrato is also used for rhythmic effects like you do with your tongue and throat. An example would be instead of doing a triplet rhythm with your tongue or throat, do it by opening and closing your hands three times a beat to give you a triplet feel. Where I first found this technique was in a book of transcribed solos. At one point in harmonica player Sonny Boy Williamson's solo the person notated a lick with triplets, but I could hear that the sound was coming from his hands and he was actually never cutting off the note with his throat or tongue. If an experienced notation artist heard that it was triplets, you know this is a strong technique.

The Double Vibrato

When doing a throat vibrato, if you open your hands in a slow rhythmic fashion it gives you the sound of an unbelievably strong pulsating vibrato. This makes for a very strong effect when you're just hanging on one note for an extended period of time.

Traditional Stylistic Techniques

Accompaniment

Traditionally acoustic style playing is not accompanied. One of the techniques used when playing acoustically is to make a background rhythm that stays dominant throughout the entire song. This is done by making two levels out of your solo. The first level is the soloistic playing itself, and the second level being the basic background rhythm that you return to when you're not soloing.

Chord Progression & Phrasing

In the traditional sense chord change doesn't happen. The whole song usually just vamps around the I Chord giving you a boogie type feel. Instead of there being chord change the harmonica player would make two to four bar phrases that give the solo unity and a sense of progression. As the twelve bar blues became standard, acoustic harmonica players just modified their playing to accommodate, but most of the same techniques still prevailed, just in a different format.

The Chug

The diatonic harmonica's note spread is laid out in chord blocks allowing a player, if he or she wants to, to play chords like an accordion. The harmonica player will usually play these chords in a chug like fashion to make the harmonica sound thick and full. The key to this technique is that your lips should always be over two or more holes and when you go to chug, your lips should never fully touch the harmonica. If your lips make a tight fit for the chug, it will sound pulled and not natural. What you're trying to accomplish is to basically just pluck the reeds and let them vibrate on their own so the effect you get is a thick chordal sound.

Tongue Blocking

One of the most dominant features about playing acoustically is the usage of tongue blocking. As stated before in the tongue blocking section tongue blocking gives you that thicker sound, and any technique that makes the harmonica sound thicker, the acoustic player will use it. The most dominant features in tongue blocking, as it applies to acoustic playing, are the tongue slap, octave, and flutter tongue. All the tongue blocking usages mentioned are used in their normal ways, but the flutter tongue is slowed down to give the rest of the notes between the octave a chance to sound.

Some Last Words About Acoustic Playing

I hope that what you just read helped you out a little bit in understanding acoustic playing. For this section I've only written down a couple of examples. Acoustic playing on the large scale would notationally be very difficult to write and read; so pay close attention to the tape for each example.

Chug Style Licks

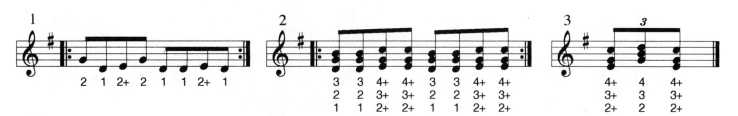

Photo Courtesy of M. Hohner Co.

SONNY TERRY / Born: October 24, 1911 - Died: March 11, 1986 / Influenced By: DeFord Bailey/Leadbelly / *Reference: Blues Who's Who*, by Sheldon Haris, March 1989 edition, pg. 502

Amplified Playing

Top Left To Right: Shure's Shallow Backed Model, Hohner Blues Blaster, Estatic JT-30, Turner Dynamic (model BD), Shure's Crystal Brown Bullet, Shure's Green Bullet. Bottom Left To Right: "Velvet Voice" Crystal, Shure SM-57, Unknown, Electro-Voice 630.

When playing amplified, the microphone and amplifier play the largest part in your sound. Your choice of microphone is probably the most important of the two. One microphone may give you a thick and full sound, and another may give you a whiny and tinny sound. The two traditional styles of microphones used the most are the straight microphones and the bullet microphones. The most popular of the two used in blues is the bullet microphone. The bullet microphone, shown above, has a large surface that fits just right in a harmonica player's cup. The bullet's face is basically flat, and unlike the ball microphone, when the bullet microphone is cupped right there is no place for sound to escape. This is important because just like your hand cup can create effects, the cup on your bullet microphone can create those same types of effects. When cupping the bullet microphone your hand holding gesture is pretty much the same as an acoustic hand cup. Your fingers should all be closed tightly together and you should leave at least one finger's distance between the face of the microphone and your harmonica. The distance between the microphone and your harmonica is important because you want to create a tone cavity just like we did with our hands for the acoustic cup. Along with the distance between the microphone and your harmonica, your cup around the harmonica must be airtight. If you were to try to blow up a balloon with a small hole in it, you'll do a lot of huffing and puffing, but you'll get nowhere because the balloon was never airtight to begin with. Just like the balloon, if your cup isn't airtight, you'll do a lot of huffing and puffing to get a tone that's not there for you. Pictures A through A3 illustrate how your hands should look while cupping your bullet microphone.

(A) The Holding Hand

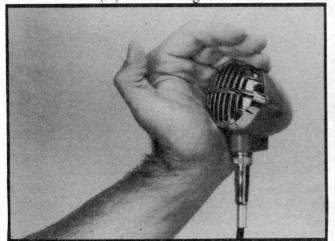

(A1) Check Your Distance From The Microphone

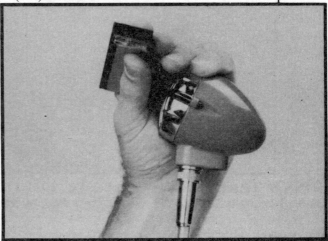

(A2) Adding Your Cupping Hand   (A3) Your Full Cup

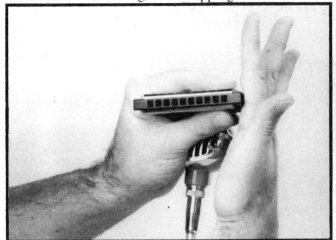
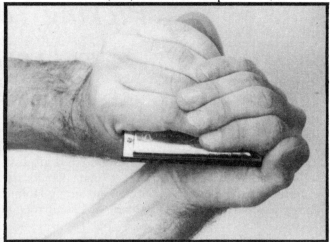

Straight Microphones

The straight microphone, like the ones used for vocals, gives you pretty much a clean and bright sound and is usually run through a P.A. system. I personally don't use the straight microphone much because I don't care for the sound it creates, and when your hands are wrapped around the microphone, sound escapes from the bottom. Because of this, you can't create the tone effects that you can with a full cup. If you can find a straight microphone with a small flat head instead of a ball, like the shaker microphone, you can use a certain amount of hand techniques. The hand techniques are minimal with these microphones, but if you experiment you might be able to find some tone effects you like. When holding a ball microphone, cup the microphone with your hands just like a normal cup, but make sure that you have your hands fully around the microphone to stop any sound from escaping.

(B) The Holding Hand   (B1) Your Full Cup

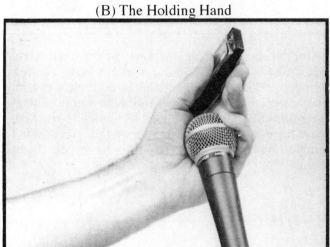
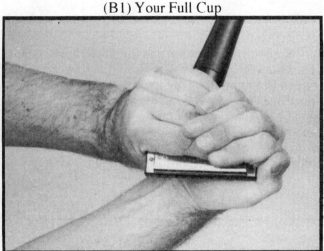

Techniques Used When Playing Amplified

When amplified, your sound and playing style on the harmonica transforms into almost a new instrument. Sounds that you couldn't hear before are suddenly brought out into the open, because of this, a new way of soloing on the harmonica emerged. More single note patterns are used and the usage of the chug style licks were thrown to the wayside. Tongue blocking is still used extensively and so are octaves, but the octaves amplified have much more of a broad effect. The 2/5 and 3/6 draw octaves are extremely powerful sounding, and the flutter tongue also sounds very full. Overall, amplified playing can be summed up by saying if you can make it sound thick, play it! If it's thin, don't.

Picking Your System

The Microphone

Almost any straight microphone can be used for the harmonica, so I'm going to concentrate on the bullet microphone. There are two elements to the bullet microphone, the body and the cartridge that picks up the sound. The first important thing about the body is how it feels in your hands, accessories like volume controls and connectors are secondary. What controls the sound is the cartridge, so if you're looking for a thick sounding microphone don't just go by what it looks like, play it! The three most favored bullet microphones by harmonica players are the Green Bullet made by Shure, the JT-30 made by Estatic, and the Blues Blaster customized by Hohner (I say customized because from what I know the Blues Blaster is just the JT-30 made by Estatic repainted blue).

Hohner's Blues Blaster	Estatic's JT-30	Shure's Green Bullet

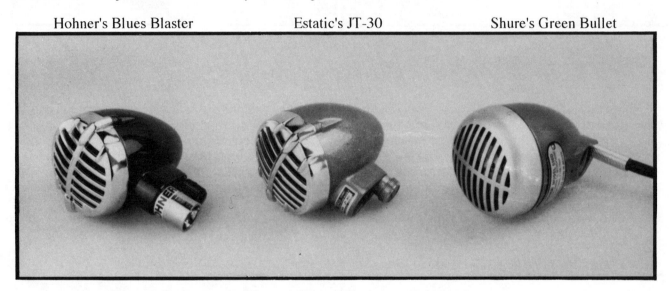

Both the Green bullet and the JT-30 have been made for decades and there are plenty of them out there. The Blues Blaster is fairly new to the market, but all three are still available on the market today. Shure's Green Bullet microphone has a magnetic cartridge, and both the Blues Blaster and the JT-30 have a crystal cartridge. My favorite of the two cartridges is the magnetic because it has a very full deep sound to it. I don't care for the sound of the crystal cartridge because I think it sounds too clean, but listen to the tape and decide which cartridge's sound you like best. If you have a preference for one or the other, don't worry about what cartridge comes with the microphone you buy, all you have to do is have your local music store order the cartridge you like and they will probably put it in for you for a small fee.

The Amplifier

The amplifiers on the market are made for guitars, there is no such thing as a harmonica amp. Because of this, harmonica players have to search high and low for the right sounding amplifier. The rule of thumb with amplifiers, in regards to the harmonica, is it has to be a tube amp. Guitar players use both solid state and tube amplifiers, the tube amplifier being the warmest and fattest sounding of the two. The biggest concern on a blues player's mind is how can I make this tinny little instrument sound big and thick, and the tube amplifier does the job very well. The next concern about your amplifier is the wattage and size of the speakers. The speaker size will usually never exceed 12" or go below 6" and the normal range of wattage will run between 25 watts and 100 watts (with exception to Fender's 12 Watt Champ). Tubes need to be driven at high wattage to get the full thick sound they're known for, so a good combination is low wattage and mid size speakers. For the harmonica player searching for an amplifier I recommend almost any fully tube Fender amplifier, or the 1993 tube reissue models from Peavey.

'59 Bassman®

'65 Twin Reverb®

~Blues Scales~

Before we get into playing anything, I would like to throw some of my findings at you. Finding one: 99% of all soloing done in blues utilizes only the notes that are found within the blues scale. Finding two: Notes found that are not in the blues scale are decorations of the blues scale, and are treated so.

Generalizing blues into theoretical concepts like I have done is a very controversial subject. A great majority of people believe that blues is a medium of expression and studying blues like a math book destroys the music. I agree that blues shouldn't be all-study, but it's just ignorance to say that the application of musical thought won't make you a better musician. A person must have complete mastery of the external aspects of music to let emotion truly shine through. When I say that 99% percent of all solos use the blues scale for their construction, I'm not saying that Little Walter had the blues scales on his mind when he wrote Juke. What I am stating is that the blues scale evolved from blues, so the blues scale is not just a scale but blues itself. I came from my mother, so I am human like my mother. The blues scale came from blues, so is the blues scale not like its mother? I hope you understand my point, because the usage's for the blues scales, if you let it, will change your life as a harmonica player.

Construction Of The Blues Scale

To help you understand how the blues scale is constructed, let's first look together at the two most dominant scales used in the western hemisphere.

The Major Scale

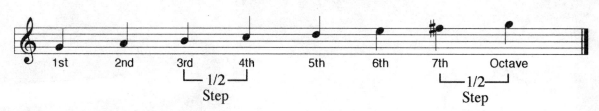

The major scale, being diatonic, uses two half steps and five whole steps for its construction. The half steps happen between the third and fourth scale degrees, and between the seventh scale degree and octave.

The Minor Scale

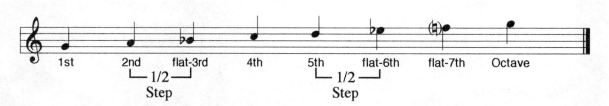

The minor scale, also being diatonic, uses two half steps and five whole steps for its construction. The half steps happen between the second and third scale degrees, and between the fifth and sixth scale degrees. The difference between the major and minor scale is the placement of the two half steps within the scale. The way these half steps in the minor scale are placed creates a darker effect.

When creating music, the notes within these scales are used for the harmony and melody. When blues is created, there is more at work than just the notes of one scale. The harmony in blues draws from both the major and minor scale, and the melody draws its note pattern from the blues scale. The blues scale itself is a melodic pattern used for soloing, and is not used like a scale in the true sense. The key idea is to think of the blues scale as a soloistic pattern that you can use to create your own solos. The top of the next page illustrates how the blues scale uses some of the same scale degrees as the minor scale.

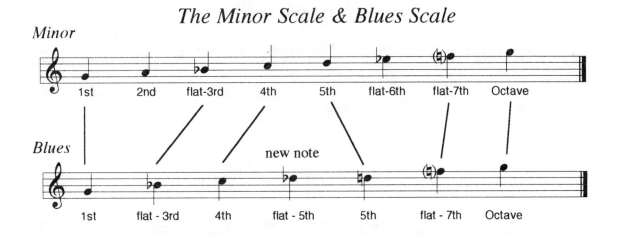

The Minor Scale & Blues Scale

As you can see, in the example above the blues scale gets most of its notes from the minor scale. The only note that doesn't come from the minor scale is the flat-5. The flat-5, along with the flat-3 and flat-7, are called **Blue Notes**. Blue notes are simply notes that are known to have a bluesy sounding quality to them. In short, if you want to sound bluesy, you play a lot of blue notes.

Getting Started

Before we start playing the blues scales we need to agree on some terminology. Traditionally each position for the harmonica has been given two names: Straight Harp aka. 1st position, Cross Harp aka. 2nd position, Draw Harp aka. 3rd position. What we're going to do is split these names into different usage's. The position itself is going to be used as the actual mode of playing its known for with its own I, IV, and V Chord. The name, like cross harp, is going to be used as the one chord relative to its position.

EX.	Playing Name	I Chord	IV Chord	V Chord
1st Position -	Straight Harp	Normal	Normal
2nd Position -	Cross Harp	Normal	Normal
3rd Position -	Draw Harp	Normal	Normal

If this is a little tough for you to understand right know, don't worry, all this will be reinforced as you play through the examples to come. On the chart above I just hinted on what these blues scales have to do with playing in the different positions. At this point we're going to concentrate on just the scales themselves and then we'll work on substituting these scales into the actual construction of the different positions.

Most Used Portions Of The Blues Scales

The actual construction of a scale starts at a given note and then ends at the octave, so that's how we're going to classify the different ranges of our harmonica, by the octave. Each blues scale has basically a three octave range, with some octaves being more complete than others. The next three examples are the most used octaves within each scale. It's very important when you read and play these scales to understand what scale degree you're on, and what it sounds like in comparison to the other notes. Having this awareness will make it easier for you to understand the concepts that are going to be taught later in this book about utilizing the blues scales. Play through each octave first to get a feel of what they sound like and then memorize the scales to the point that you can one: play the scales by memory and two: recite each note and its corresponding scale degree on the harmonica that corresponds to the blues scale in question. This might seem like a lot, but as I stated before, you must have complete mastery of the external influences of music to let your emotions truly shine through.

Cross Harp Blues Scale

| | 2 | 3' | 4+ | 4' | 4 | 5 | 6+ | 6+ | 5 | 4 | 4' | 4+ | 3' | 2 |

┌── 1st   flat - 3rd   4th   flat - 5th   5th   flat - 7th   Octave

Scale
Degrees

Straight Harp Blues Scale

| 1+ | 2+ | 2" | 2' | 2 | 3' | 4+ | 4+ | 3' | 2 | 2' | 2" | 2+ | 1+ |

1st   (Natural - 3)   4th   flat - 5th   5th   flat - 7th   Octave

Draw Harp Blues Scale

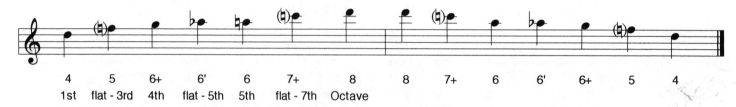

| 4 | 5 | 6+ | 6' | 6 | 7+ | 8 | 8 | 7+ | 6 | 6' | 6+ | 5 | 4 |

1st   flat - 3rd   4th   flat - 5th   5th   flat - 7th   Octave

For the blues scales above, all of them were complete except one. In the first position blues scale the flat third isn't available, because there is no bend possible on the 2 blow. The flat-3, being one of the blue notes, is an important part of the blues scale and without the third scale degree being flatted you can hear how much less bluesy the scale sounds compared to the cross harp and draw harp blues scale. Let's go on now to look at the full range of each blues scale. What we're trying to look for is a fully usable blues scale for each of the three octaves on our harmonica. The next three examples show all of these blues scales in order from the bottom octave to the top octave. If a note is not available, there will be an "NA" printed in its place. Below each hole number that is a blue note, there will be a "B" notated. If a blue note is not available, there will be an "NA" printed in its place. (Have you memorized the bends available to you yet!)

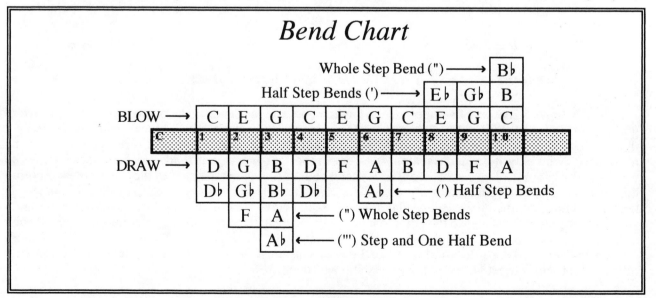

Bend Chart

Octave Placement For Cross Harp

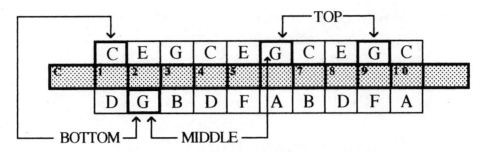

Cross Harp Blues Scales

Octave Placement For Draw Harp

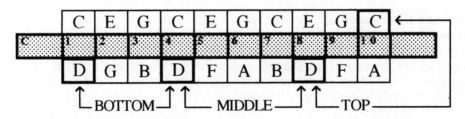

Draw Harp Blues Scales

Octave Placement For Straight Harp

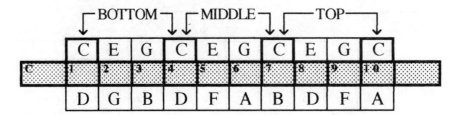

Straight Harp Blues Scales

BOTTOM OCTAVE	MIDDLE OCTAVE	TOP OCTAVE
Incomplete	Not Available	~ Complete ~

I hope you caught all that, it's a lot to swallow at first. Let's now make some generalizations about what you just read. I said that a solo can't happen without the presence of the blues scale, so each octave on our harmonica must have a majority of the notes within the blues scale to be applicable.

About The Cross Harp Blues Scales

Looking at the cross harp blues scale, the one octave that has a complete blues scale is in the middle, starting at the 2 draw and ending on the 6 blow. The cross harp middle octave is the most used part of our harmonica when playing blues and country. To play bluesy you must use bends, and the middle octave is riddled with them. The bottom cross harp octave is complete until it drops out two notes early, missing the flat-3 and root note. The bottom octave, even though it's not complete, is used a lot in soloing also due to the availability of bends. The top cross harp octave is fairly complete, but is missing two of its blue notes, making bluesy playing tough. Overall the cross harp blues scale is the most widely used because of all the bends that are available.

About The Draw Harp And Straight Harp Blues Scales

Looking at the draw harp blues scale, there are two complete octaves of the blues scale available to you. The hardest of the two blues scales is the bottom octave because of all the articulate bends it asks for. The top blues scale just misses the octave by one note, but the scale itself is missing two out of the three blue notes, so it to is also hard to play bluesy. Looking at the straight harp blues scale, there are almost two complete octaves of the blues scale available to you. The bottom barely doesn't make a blues scale because the flat-3 isn't available, but even though the bottom blues scale isn't complete, it is used the most. The reason why it's used the most is because the other complete octave is on the high end and uses blow bends for its construction. Blow bends in the first place are tough to play articulate, and to use blow bends in a musical context is even tougher. The middle octave, being where there is basically no bends, is pretty much unusable because of the lack of any blue notes. Again, memorize each octave in all the blues scales because the chapters to come utilize the techniques available in these blues scales.

~Octave Substitution~

One of the greatest techniques you'll ever do with the blues scales is to use them for octave substitution. Octave substitution is the most powerful tool you could use to get familiar with every part of your harmonica. Octave substitution simply uses licks from your harmonica that you already know, and transposes them to other octaves for you to play.

Cross Harp Octave Substitutions

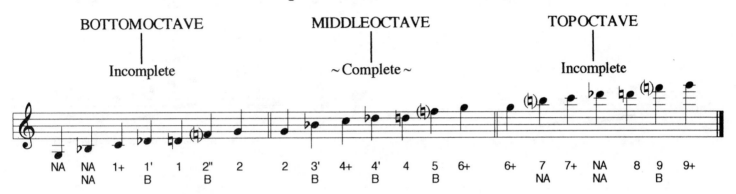

Transposing Middle Octave Licks To The Bottom Octave

The one complete blues scale for the full cross harp blues scales is the middle octave. The bottom octave is complete until it drops off at the bottom, missing the flat-3 and root note. When transposing a lick from the middle octave to the bottom octave, the lick shouldn't pass below the 4th scale degree which is the 4 blow. Since the middle octave starts on the 6 blow, the example below will only use the notes between the 6 blow and 4 blow for its construction.

Transposing Bottom And Middle Octave Licks To The Top Octave

The top octave is fairly complete, but the third scale degree is not lowerable making the flat-3 not available, and the flat-5 is completely missing from this scale. If you were to transpose licks from the middle octave to the high octave they shouldn't have a 4 draw bend or half-step 3 draw bend in them. Licks using the 3 draw can be used, but remember that the bent 3 draw is a blue note and an unbent 3 draw will give you a lighter feel in your solos. To transpose licks from your bottom octave the only note you can't use would be the 1 draw bend (1 draw and 4 draw are both the same notes in octaves). The examples on the next page show middle octave licks that don't use the 4 draw bend or 3 draw half-step bend, and bottom octave licks without the 1 draw bend, so they can be transposed to the high end.

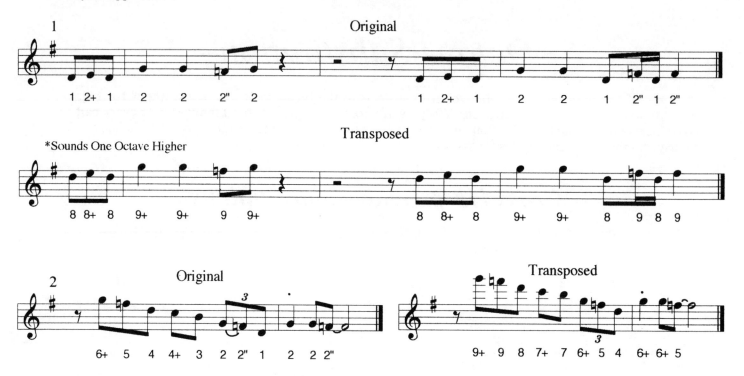

Transposing Top Octave Licks To The Middle And Bottom Octave

Since the middle octave is complete, any lick on the high end can be played on the middle octave. Any high end lick can be transferred to the bottom octave as long as the high end lick doesn't go below the 7 blow.

Draw Harp Octave Substitutions

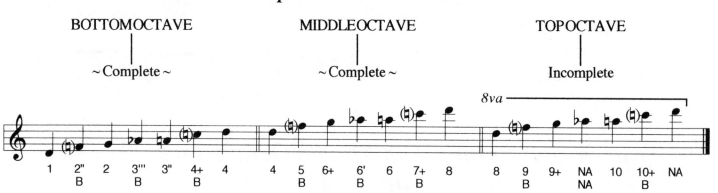

There really isn't much that can be said about draw harp octave substitution because there are two full octaves of the blues scale, and the top octave is only missing two notes. Since both the middle and bottom octaves are complete blues scales, any lick that can be used on one, can be used on the other. If you were to substitute licks to the high end, you would have to make sure that they don't have the flat-5 or root at the octave. The top of the next page gives an example of what type of licks can be transposed to the high end.

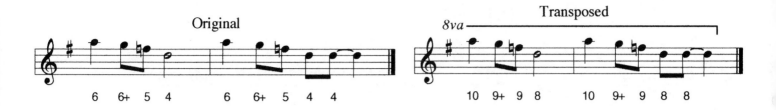

Original   Transposed

6   6+   5   4   6   6+   5   4   4   10   9+   9   8   10   9+   9   8   8

Straight Harp Octave Substitution

BOTTOM OCTAVE	MIDDLE OCTAVE	TOP OCTAVE
Incomplete	Not Available	~ Complete ~

1+   2+   2"   2'   2   3'   4+   4+   5+   5   NA   6+   7   7+   7+   8'+   9   9'+   9+   10"+   10+
     NA   B   B   NA   NA   NA   B   B   B

Looking at the straight harp blues scale, there are almost two complete octaves of the blues scale available to you. The bottom almost makes a blues scale but the flat-3 isn't available, but even though the bottom blues scale isn't complete, it is used the most. The middle octave, being where there are basically no bends, is pretty much unusable because of the lack of any blue notes. Since the only difference between the top octave and the bottom octave is that you can't get a flat-3 on the low end, basically any lick can be used for octave substitution.

Some Last Words About Using Octave Substitution For Increasing Your Range

This chapter may take a couple read throughs to get the whole gist of what I said, but this technique is well worth it. If you're a player who says that you're not good at playing the extremities of your harmonica, this is your chance to shine. Reading through the last three chapters you might have found that 3rd position has surprisingly a lot available to you. believe it or not 3rd position has more of the blues scale available to you on the I Chord than 2nd position does. Now that you know what 3rd position is all about, I hope you'll have as much fun playing in it as I do.

Using Octave Substitution In A Solo

When I developed the technique octave substitution I originally meant it to be a way for players to get use to the extremities of their harmonica, but I have found that it also works great in a solo when used in conjunction with phrasing. To try this technique, play a lick in the middle range of your harmonica that can be transposed up to the high or low end. By playing the original lick first you'll set up the octave substitution, making the transposed lick add unity to your solo. I like to change the transposed lick a little bit to add variance, usually to set-up the chord change. The example on the next page shows how this technique can be used in a solo with the original lick marked with an "O" and the transposed lick marked with a "T". I recommend for you to read how phrasing works in section 3 to get a better understanding of how I'm using this technique in the solo.

Phrasing And Octave Substitution

~Playing Positions~

Part One: Form

Before we get into the meat of playing in the different positions let's first examine together the form, or structure of blues. I want you to think of the structure of music as a house. The foundation of the house is the rhythm, the walls are the harmony, the roof is the melody, and the building material the form. As you can see, each structural element depends upon the other. The element we now want to concentrate on is the form. Without exception, every musical composition has a discernible organizing principle, or structure that it follows. Form gives writers a mold for the shaping of their musical compositions. For hundreds of years classical composers have used such forms as binary, ternary, rondo, and sonata. These forms modulate to new key centers and explore rhythmic, harmonic, and melodic complexities. Let's now look at how blues works within a form. A major principle of formal organization in the construction of classical works is repetition and contrast. Blues bases its form upon this principle. Classical compositions have reoccurring melodies for repetition and explores new key areas for contrast. Blues uses the repetition of a twelve bar pattern and you as the soloist make the contrast. This twelve bar form is a repeated chord progression that utilizes three chords in a major and minor key context. 99% of all your soloing will be done above this 12 bar blues progression.

12 Bar Blues

The twelve bar blues progression utilizes three main chords: the one chord (I), the four chord (IV), and the five chord (V). These chords are built upon the first, fourth, and fifth scale degrees of the diatonic scale. This diatonic scale is what the ten hole harmonica is based upon, thus the name diatonic harmonica. This scale uses seven scale degrees as shown below.

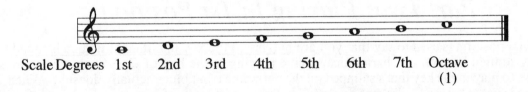

| Scale Degrees | 1st | 2nd | 3rd | 4th | 5th | 6th | 7th | Octave |

(1)

Notice that the scale starts on one and ends on one. Just as when you start to count you start with the number one, when music starts, it starts on the one chord (I). The I Chord is the home base in a song. In most songs you'll start on the I Chord, and when the song is over, it will finish on the I Chord.

What Are Chords?

A chord is a vertical structure created when three or more notes are struck simultaneously (all at the same time), or arpeggiated (one right after the other). These chords are built with three or four notes in thirds. For example: If you strike the first, third and fifth scale degrees at the same time you'll get a I Chord. If you strike the second, fourth, and sixth scale degrees at the same time you'll get a II Chord. If you keep on stacking these scale degrees, you'll find that it finishes with the same notes that it started with, the I Chord.

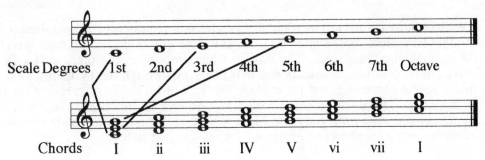

| Scale Degrees | 1st | 2nd | 3rd | 4th | 5th | 6th | 7th | Octave |

| Chords | I | ii | iii | IV | V | vi | vii | I |

As stated before, twelve bar blues is based upon chords that are built on the first, fourth, and fifth scale degrees. <u>These chords are what the band is playing beneath you to support your solo.</u> This a very important concept that you need to understand, as a soloist, you have to work with what is thrown at you from the band. Common sense tells us that if the band dictates what we solo above, we better be well acquainted with what they're playing.

12 Bar Blues

The 12 bar blues format is a twelve measure progression that is repeated until the song ends. Within these twelve bars are three chords that are placed in predetermined places within the progression to give variety within the song. The 12 bar blues progression is illustrated below.

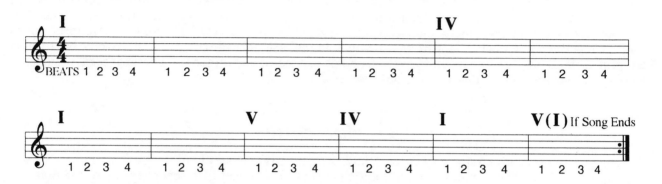

Part Two: Playing In 1st Position

The term 1st position is used to say that you are <u>playing in the key that the harmonica is tuned to</u>. If you're playing straight harp on a C harmonica, you're playing in the key of C. I know this sounds like common sense to play in the key that's stamped on the harmonica, but blues actually doesn't. When I say that something is in the key of C, I'm stating that C is the central pitch of importance. When you play a song in the key of C, it will start and then end with that pitch. This note that the scale starts with is called your **tonic**. The tonic of a key is your home base, so if you say you're playing in the key of x, your stating that x is your tonic. As stated before, twelve bar blues is based upon chords that are built on the first, fourth, and fifth scale degrees. Using the key of C lets look at what notes are in the I, IV, and V Chord.

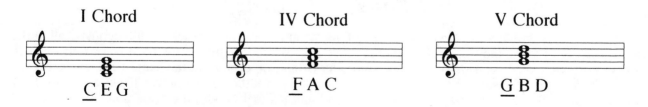

The root notes of each of those chords tell us what blues scales that we can use. Remembering back to the blues scales the straight harp blues scale started on C, so any time you're on the I Chord, you'll use a lick that fits within the straight harp blues scale. The IV Chord has a root of F, but there isn't a IV Chord blues scale available to us in 1st position, so usually you will just play through the IV Chord as if it were the I Chord. This might sound confusing, but I'll explain this I Chord, IV Chord substitution after we discuss the rest of the positions. The V Chord starts with a root note of G, this is the same note that the cross harp blues scale starts with. Any time you're on the V Chord in 1st position, you'll use cross harp style licks. The chart on the next page shows an example of what was just stated.

1st Position Soloing

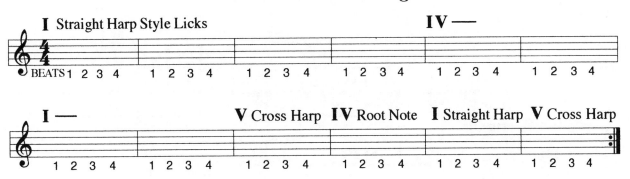

1st Position Generalizations

1st position is generally used for playing folk style music because tunes naturally fall well on the harmonica in straight harp. When we went over the straight harp blues scale you could see how hard it was to make a complete blues scale. The problem with 1st position is that you have to spend seven bars on the I Chord, and since the straight harp blues scale is what you use for the I Chord, 1st position playing can be tricky to make sound good. The good news is the most usable blues scale, the cross harp blues scale, is on the V Chord, but the bad news is the V Chord only happens for two bars in the 12 bar blues progression. The IV Chord also carries some problems because of the lack of a blues scale, so overall 1st position isn't a great position to play in if you want to sound bluesy. The best thing I feel the 1st position playing has to offer is the high end blues scale. High notes tickle the ears of the people listening and anything you can play in a position that has a full blues scale in it, you can play it on the high end by position substitution. Position substitution will be covered thoroughly in the next chapter.

Part Three: Playing In 2nd Position

When we play in 2nd position, we are actually changing the tonic to a new pitch, thus giving us a new key and scale to work within. The question this brings up is "why do we want to play in a key that the harmonica was originally never meant to be played in?" When playing blues, the most predominant features are <u>bends and blue notes</u>. As stated before, bending adds expression and blue notes are particular notes that sound bluesy. When playing in 1st position, you're spending most of your time on the blows, because the blows fit well within that key. When playing in 2nd position, you're spending most of your time on the draws, thus making bends and blue notes readily available to you. Look at the charts below and compare the versatility of the draw side to the blow side.

Bend Chart

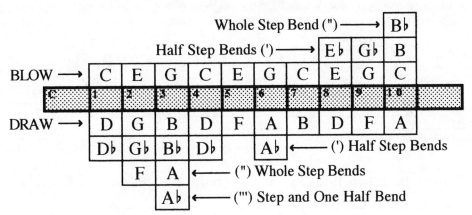

Blue Notes

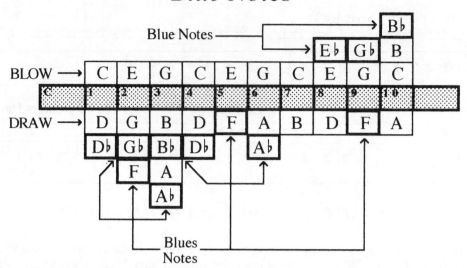

Looking at the bend chart, there are four blow bends available and eight draw bends available. Bend wise, the draw side has twice as many bends available to you. Looking at the blue note chart, there are three blow blue notes available and nine draw blue notes available. For blue notes, the draw side has triple the blue notes available to you. The objective in playing 2nd position is to make our home base on the draw side so all the blue notes and bends are available to us at will.

The Relation Between
1st position And 2nd Position

Position	Key	I Chord	IV Chord	V Chord
1st	C	C	(F)	G
2nd	G	G	C	(D)

Looking at the note chart above you can see the only difference between 1st position playing and 2nd position playing is one root note (remember that the root note determines the blues scale that is used). Both positions use the straight harp (C) and cross harp blues scale (G), but in 2nd position the draw harp blues scale is also used (D). The differences also lay in the placement of these blues scales. In 2nd position playing the most usable blues scale, the cross harp blues scale, is now the I Chord. The draw harp blues scale, now being on the V Chord, makes every chord in 2nd position have a full blues scale on it. The 12 bar blues progression, below, shows the placement of these blues scales for your 2nd position solos.

2nd Position Soloing

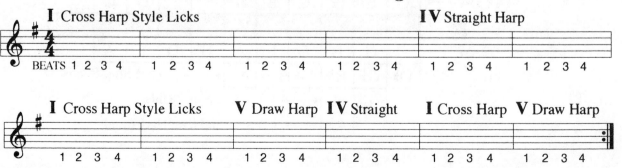

2nd Position Generalizations

Overall this is the most usable, and most used position for the harmonica. Most people using this book are probably 2nd position players. If you play mostly in 2nd position don't overlook what you just read, the blues scales themselves aren't just scales, but really cool bluesy sounding riffs. Take this new way of thinking about your solos and try to bridge some of your high end licks with your low end licks, you'll find you can get some pretty cool riffs that encompass the entire harmonica.

Part Four: Playing In 3rd Position

3rd position is probably the most misunderstood position out of the three. 3rd position has twice as many soloing possibilities available than 1st position does, yet there are still people that play 1st position more than they do 3rd. In fact only about 1/6 of all professional harmonica players can really say that they can solo in 3rd position well. I feel this is because players don't understand 3rd position, but kind of understand 1st. The draw harp blues scale has two full blues scales available, one being on the low end and the other on the mid to high range of the harmonica. My favorite part of the draw harp blues scale is the 4 draw to the 8 draw. This part of the scale is just high enough to tickle peoples ears and you don't have to do many high end bends. Not having to do any bends for the scale is important because high notes that have to be bent need to be perfectly in tune to sound good.

The Relation Between
2nd position And 3rd Position

Position	Key	I Chord	IV Chord	V Chord
2nd	G	G	Ⓒ	D
3rd	D	D	G	Ⓐ

Statistics state that you're probably a 2nd position player, and if you are, 3rd position should be a piece of cake for you to learn. When on the I Chord in 3rd position what you need to think about is what you would normally play on the V Chord in 2nd position. Since the draw harp blues scale is only used twice in 2nd position for the V Chord, it will take you a little while to get comfortable spending so much time on the draw harp blues scale in 3rd position. The IV Chord in 3rd position uses the same blues scale as the I chord in 2nd position, the cross harp blues scale. So soloing on the IV Chord should bring no problems either. The V Chord uses a new pitch that we haven't dealt with yet, that note is A on the C harmonica (always keep in mind we're using a C harmonica for illustration purposes and the notes will change for different keyed harmonicas, but the scales remain the same). When I illustrated the 12 bar progression for 1st position soloing (pg. 49), on the second presentation of the IV Chord I put an indication to play the root note of the chord. In soloing terms it's common to play a root note over a chord that only happens for one measure. the root note sends a message of agreement with the band and it's a nice rest for the listeners ears from an active solo. When playing the V Chord in 3rd position I recommend to just use the root note. The root notes available to you are on the 6 draw, 10 draw, and 3 draw whole step bend. I like to play the 6 draw root note on the V Chord and then resolve downward to the 6 blow root note for the IV Chord; this makes for a nice root oriented progression. On top of the next page is the 12 bar solo pattern for playing in 3rd position.

3rd Position Soloing

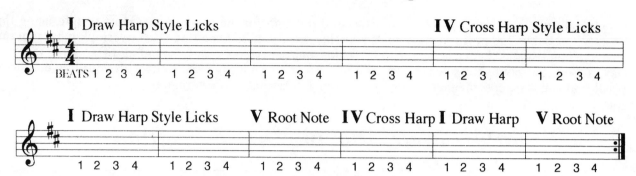

3rd Position Generalizations

3rd position is one of my favorite position to solo in, second to 2nd position of course. 3rd position adds great contrast to your solos and I guarantee if you work with 3rd position it will become one of your favorite positions.

About Key Relations & Extended Positions

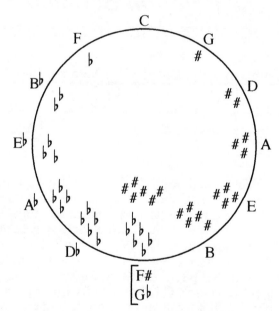

What you see written above is called the *Circle Of Fifths*. This circle shows all the keys available in the diatonic realm. As harmonica players, we don't need to know all the different keys because when we want to play in a different key we just pick up a different keyed harmonica. The one thing we do need to be aware of is how these different keys effect us when we are playing in the different positions. When we change to a different position we are actually playing in a different key. If you have a C harmonica and your playing in 1st position, your playing in the key of C. If you have a C harmonica and your playing in 2nd position, your actually playing in the key of G. If you have a C harmonica and your playing in 3rd position, your playing in the key of D. All of these keys are fifth relations, look at the chart above and start with C and go to the right, you'll see that G follows C, and D follows G.

The reason why you're able to play in the different keys with one harmonica is because of the relations between the keys themselves. When playing blues the 3rd, 5th, and 7th scale degrees are flatted to give you the blue notes. When doing so, you negate up to two sharps in the key signature, that's why we can play up to two sharps past the original key of the harmonica. If you go past the two sharps you start getting some dissonance's between you and the band that doesn't sit well with the music. This brings up the question, "Are there more positions than three?" In a conceptual way, yes there are more than three positions. Some people have gone as far to say that there is a playable position for each key. Positions other than the three that I have mentioned are usually used if they happen to fit a particular well known song that was originally written for an instrument other than the harmonica. The whole reason for playing in other positions is to add versatility to your solos, but each of those positions had at least two of the I, IV, and V Chord blues scales available to you; the other positions can't offer you that, so other positions are reserved for songs with a special purpose in mind. The key word is experiment!

Finding What Key Your Playing In For Each Position

Using the C harmonica again as an example, what we need to look for is an octave of the I Chord blues scale and look at the starting note of the scale to find your key. In 1st position we use the straight harp blues scale as our I Chord. Looking at the bottom octave it starts on a 1 blow and ends on the 4 blow, both the 4 blow and 1 blow are a C. That tells us that the key we are playing in while playing 1st position on the C harmonica is the key of C. In 2nd position we use the cross harp blues scale as our I Chord. Looking at the middle octave it starts on a 2 draw and ends on the 6 blow, both the 2 draw and 6 blow are a G. That tells us that the key we are playing in while playing 2nd position on the C harmonica is the key of G. In 3rd position we use the draw harp blues scale as our I Chord. Looking at the middle octave it starts on a 4 draw and ends on the 8 draw, both the 4 draw and 8 draw are a D. That tells us that the key we are playing in while playing 3rd position on the C harmonica is the key of D.

An Even Quicker Way To Find Your Key

When playing in 1st position, look at the note on your 1 blow, that is your key
When playing in 2nd position, look at the note on your 2 draw, that is your key
When playing in 3rd position, look at the note on your 4 draw, that is your key

EX.   D Harmonica

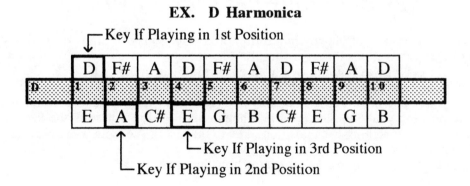

Some Last Words About Soloing In Positions

My last word is we're not done with positions yet. The coming chapters will help you reinforce some of the things you read about in this chapter. Positions can be very rewarding if you apply yourself, but like everything good, your going to have to do some hard work and digging. This book is not intended to be the last word. All of the wonderful things in this section I have shown you so far are meant to give you new ideas and insight on the soloing you have already been doing. What I'm teaching isn't my style, but ideas you can develop in your style.

~Position Substitution~

Position substitution is very similar to octave substitution in the respect that in both techniques your using licks you already know to further your lick vocabulary on ranges of the harmonica you're not so familiar with. Position substitution is the act of taking a lick or passage from a solo in one position, and translates it into another position. Before we go further into position substitution, I want to make sure that you completely understand the key relations that happen between positions. The example below is from page 53, chapter 10.

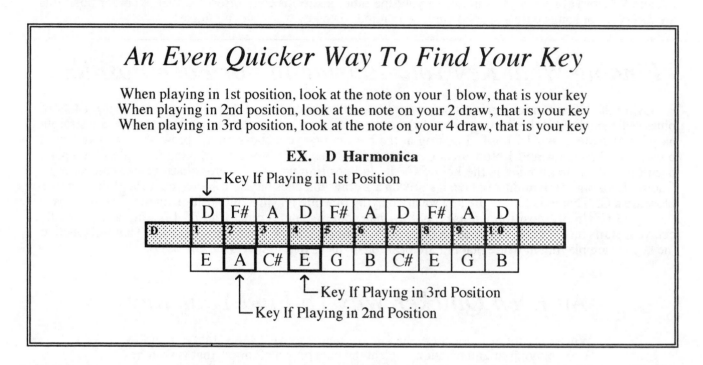

An Even Quicker Way To Find Your Key

When playing in 1st position, look at the note on your 1 blow, that is your key
When playing in 2nd position, look at the note on your 2 draw, that is your key
When playing in 3rd position, look at the note on your 4 draw, that is your key

EX. D Harmonica

┌ Key If Playing in 1st Position

| D | F# | A | D | F# | A | D | F# | A | D |

| E | A | C# | E | G | B | C# | E | G | B |

└ Key If Playing in 3rd Position
└ Key If Playing in 2nd Position

Key Relations Between Positions

So far we have only thought of playing in positions as a way to play in other keys. It's very common for a musician to change positions during a song to add variety. I'm sure you've seen a performance where the harmonica player was holding two or three harmonicas in his hand, what he was doing was changing positions during the breaks and solos. The diagram above uses a D harmonica as an example of the different keys you're playing in for each of the three positions. When in 2nd position you're in the key of A, when in 3rd position you're in the key of E, when in 1st position you're in the key of D. The way we're able to do this is by matching each position's key to the key of the song we're playing in. For us to play in the different positions around <u>one key center</u> what we want to do is make the 1 blow, 2 draw, and 4 draw the same key. The next three diagrams show how this is achieved.

"E" Harmonica In 1st Position

┌ Key in 1st Position

| E | G# | B | E | G# | B | E | G# | B | E |

| F# | B | D# | F# | A | C# | D# | F# | A | C# |

"A" Harmonica In 2nd Position

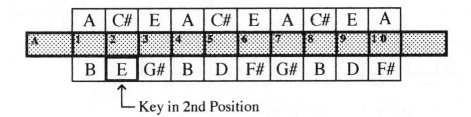

	A	C#	E	A	C#	E	A	C#	E	A	
A	1	2	3	4	5	6	7	8	9	10	
	B	E	G#	B	D	F#	G#	B	D	F#	

↑ Key in 2nd Position

"D" Harmonica In 3rd Position

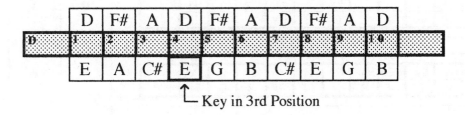

	D	F#	A	D	F#	A	D	F#	A	D	
D	1	2	3	4	5	6	7	8	9	10	
	E	A	C#	E	G	B	C#	E	G	B	

↑ Key in 3rd Position

What all three harmonicas, in each of their separate positions, had in common was the key in which they were being played. All the harmonicas were being played in the key of E. By doing this, you can switch positions at will just by picking up the corresponding harmonica for each position. On the next page is a position chart that shows all the keys and their relative positions. When trying to find all the positions that correspond to one key, look down the right column for the same letter name. For example: If you wanted to find the three harmonicas that are used in each position for the key of D, you would use a C harmonica in 3rd position, a G harmonica in 2nd position, and a D harmonica in 1st position. The other key thing about this chart is it has the complete note spread for each key of the harmonica. If you're more visually oriented you'll want to use this note spread for octave substitution and position substitution.

Using Octave Substitution

The first thing you need to do is classify which of the positions is the easiest for you to solo in, and which of the positions is the hardest for you to solo in. You're going to want to start with the position that's easiest for you to solo in, and use that position for all of the licks you're going to transfer to the other positions. For most people 2nd position is the easiest, so we're going to start there. What we want to look for is a complete blues scale to transfer to, so we'll use the bottom and top octaves of the straight harp blues scale in 1st position and the middle octave draw harp blues scale in 3rd position (I know that the bottom octave in 1st position is missing the blue note on the 3rd scale degree, but like I stated before more people are used to the bottom octave of the straight harp blues scale).

Transferring 2nd Position Licks To 3rd Position

On the cross harp blues scale the middle and bottom octave licks are used the most, so we'll use that note range for the licks we're going to transfer to the draw harp blues scale. In the draw harp blues scale the bottom and middle octaves have complete blues scale on them. So when we transfer licks to the draw harp blues scale we'll use that range. We're going to use a D harmonica in 2nd position and a G harmonica in 3rd position, this makes your key center A. By doing this, all the licks we transferred will have the same pitch content, in other terms they will sound the same between positions.

Harmonica Position Chart

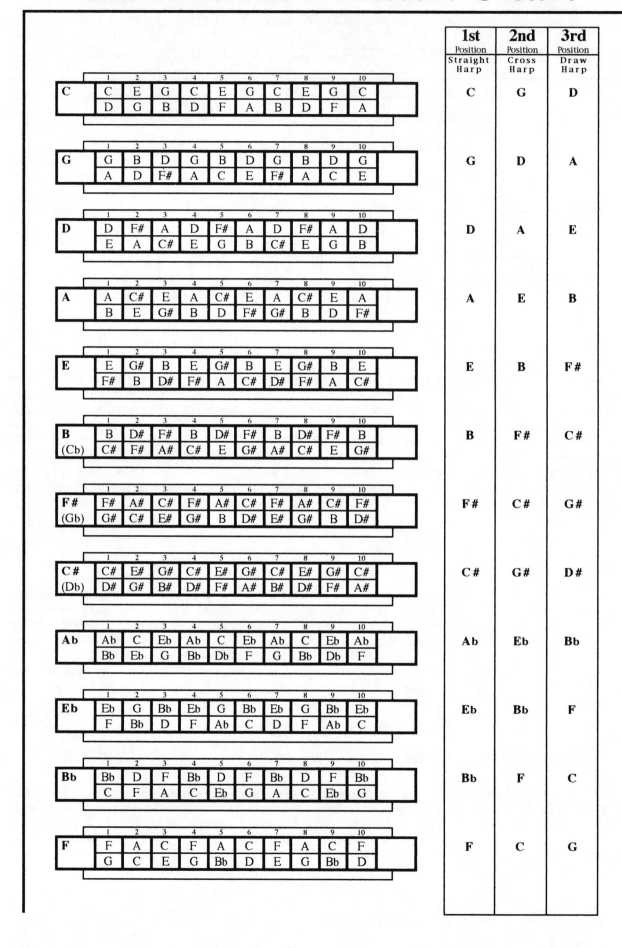

Harp	1	2	3	4	5	6	7	8	9	10	1st Position Straight Harp	2nd Position Cross Harp	3rd Position Draw Harp
C	C / D	E / G	G / B	C / D	E / F	G / A	C / B	E / D	G / F	C / A	C	G	D
G	G / A	B / D	D / F#	G / A	B / C	D / E	G / F#	B / A	D / C	G / E	G	D	A
D	D / E	F# / A	A / C#	D / E	F# / G	A / B	D / C#	F# / E	A / G	D / B	D	A	E
A	A / B	C# / E	E / G#	A / B	C# / D	E / F#	A / G#	C# / B	E / D	A / F#	A	E	B
E	E / F#	G# / B	B / D#	E / F#	G# / A	B / C#	E / D#	G# / F#	B / A	E / C#	E	B	F#
B (Cb)	B / C#	D# / F#	F# / A#	B / C#	D# / E	F# / G#	B / A#	D# / C#	F# / E	B / G#	B	F#	C#
F# (Gb)	F# / G#	A# / C#	C# / E#	F# / G#	A# / B	C# / D#	F# / E#	A# / G#	C# / B	F# / D#	F#	C#	G#
C# (Db)	C# / D#	E# / G#	G# / B#	C# / D#	E# / F#	G# / A#	C# / B#	E# / D#	G# / F#	C# / A#	C#	G#	D#
Ab	Ab / Bb	C / Eb	Eb / G	Ab / Bb	C / Db	Eb / F	Ab / G	C / Bb	Eb / Db	Ab / F	Ab	Eb	Bb
Eb	Eb / F	G / Bb	Bb / D	Eb / F	G / Ab	Bb / C	Eb / D	G / F	Bb / Ab	Eb / C	Eb	Bb	F
Bb	Bb / C	D / F	F / A	Bb / C	D / Eb	F / G	Bb / A	D / C	F / Eb	Bb / G	Bb	F	C
F	F / G	A / C	C / E	F / G	A / Bb	C / D	F / E	A / G	C / Bb	F / D	F	C	G

Transferring 2nd Position Licks To 3rd Position

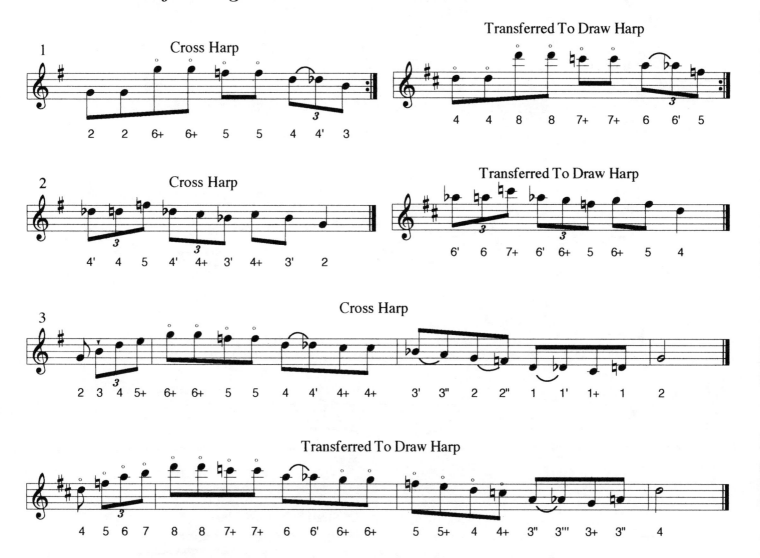

As you can see, any lick that can be done on the cross harp blues scale can be done on the draw harp blues scale. The one problem you might face is when transferring your cross harp licks to draw harp, the key for the harmonica in draw harp might be too high for you to do bends well. As you try some of your licks on different keys you'll find which keys work well for you. I want to remind you one more time that even when we change keys of harmonica the notation will stay constant in C, G, and D. This helps with the reading of the music and as long as you understand that the notes change when you change keys we'll be fine.

Transferring 2nd Position Licks To 1st Position

Transferring licks to the straight harp blues scale is tricky. The high end is the only part of the scale that is complete, but there are many articulate blow bends in its construction. The bottom is just missing the blue note on the 2 blow, so for illustration purposes we're going to use both the top and bottom straight harp blues scales. If you're not good at the high blow bends yet just skip over the part where the lick is transferred to the top octave for now, but remember to go back to them when you get better with the blow bends. The examples on the next page use a D harmonica in 2nd position and an A harmonica in 1st position. This puts your central pitch at A. If the 1st position key is too high for you, just play the tape to get an idea of what the lick sounds like and then pick two keys of a lower register. Each cross harp style lick will be transferred to both bottom and top octaves of the straight harp blues scale.

Transferring 2nd Position Licks To 1st Position

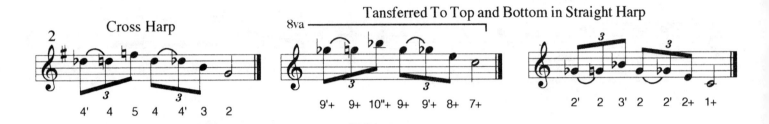

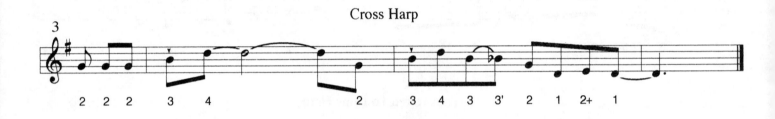

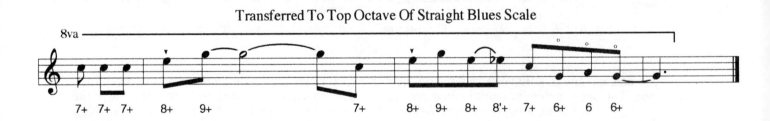

Some Last Words About The Blues Scales And Their Substitutions

Looking at examples 1, 2, and 3 you can see that there's quite a few licks that can be used for substitution. As long as you stay within the blues scale, you can pretty much transfer anything to the high end in 1st position. Now that you have transferred new licks into 1st and 3rd position, you can take those same licks and move them around to other octaves in the blues scale using octave substitution. You'll find that the techniques from the last four chapters work together very well in helping you get a larger lick vocabulary and more proficient at soloing in other positions.

Before going into more examples of position substitution I would like to give you a chart easier to read than the ones shown in chapter 8. Written below are each of the blues scales with all the notes that they have available to you. When getting use to playing around the blues scale this is probably the easiest chart to use. The next example is a solo that uses all three positions within the same key. Each lick that will be used for each solo will be substituted from the first 2nd position solo, with exception to some stylistic differences between positions. The central key of this song is the key of A. The harmonicas that we will be using are the: D harmonica in 2nd position, G harmonica in 3rd position, and A harmonica in 1st position. When first trying to learn this song remember that my purpose in each example is that they are meant to be just as much as an exercise as a song to play along with. This song isn't easy, so take it slow and play each bar as a separate exercise, then put the song together into a cohesive whole. As you play through this example remember that If you were to switch positions within a song you could use exact repeats of the solo before in small bits to give the song unity; it also works well for phrasing.

A Quick Way Of Looking At The Blues Scales

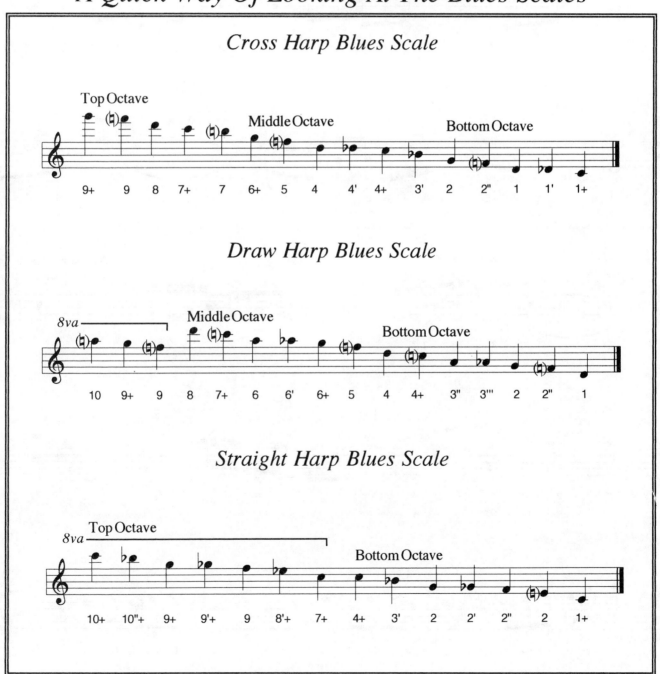

59

Using Position Substitution Around One Central Pitch

"D" Harmonica in 2nd Position

2 3   4   4' 4+ 3' 2   2   2   3' 4+ 4' 4   5   5
               1+   2   2

6+ 5 4 4' 4+ 3' 2   3'   4' 4+ 3' 4+ 3' 2   2   4' 4+ 3' 4+ 3' 2   2" 1 1'

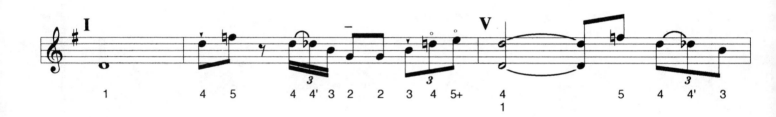

1   4 5   4 4' 3 2   2 3 4 5+   4   5 4 4' 3
                                           1

"G" Harmonica
in 3rd Position

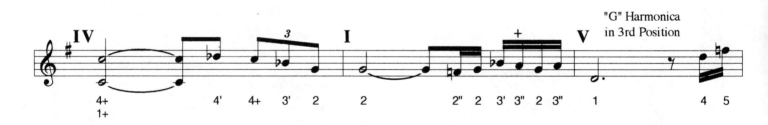

4+   4' 4+ 3' 2   2   2" 2 3' 3" 2 3"   1   4 5
1+

6   6' 6+ 5 4   4   4 5 6+ 6' 6   7+   7+
          3+   4+   4+

8 7+ 6 6' 6+ 5 4   5   6' 6+ 5 6+ 5 4   4   6' 6+ 5 6+ 5 4   4+ 3" 3'''

I

3"   6 7+ 6 6' 5 4 4 5 6 7 6   7+ 6 6' 5

IV   I   V   "A" Harmonica in 1st Position

6+   6' 6+ 5 4 4   4+ 4 5 5+ 4 5+ 6   7+ 8+
3+

*All notes sound one octave higher than written

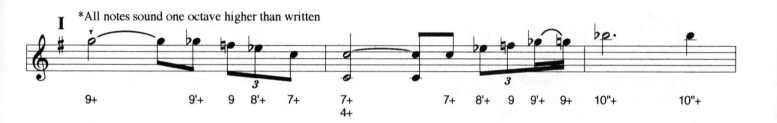

I

9+   9'+ 9 8'+ 7+ 7+   7+ 8'+ 9 9'+ 9+ 10"+   10"+
            4+

             IV

10+ 10"+ 9+ 9'+ 9 8'+ 7+ 8'+ 9'+ 9 8'+ 9 8'+ 7+ 7+ 9'+ 9 8'+ 9 8'+ 7+ 6 6'

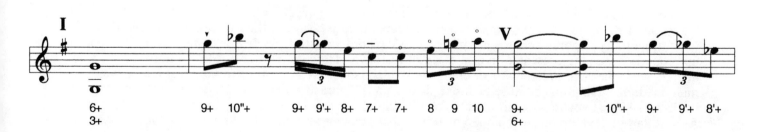

I   V

6+   9+ 10"+ 9+ 9'+ 8+ 7+ 7+ 8 9 10 9+   10"+ 9+ 9'+ 8'+
3+   6+

              "D" Harmonica in 2nd Position

IV   I

9   9'+ 9 8'+ 7+ 7+ 6+ 5 4 4+ 2 3' 3" 2 2 2 2' 2"
5   4+

 Soloing Techniques

As a harmonica player whenever you're asked to play something, you're put in a soloing situation. It might take a person who plays an orchestral instrument three or more years before he or she even begins to study how to solo. Even then, if they have a solo, it's written down for them and it's guaranteed to match the orchestra and sound good as long as they play the notes with a certain degree of proficiency. Since we play an instrument that isn't given that type of forum, we are left to make up our own solos, usually on the spot. As an instructor I have players come to me that have a great deal of proficiency on the harmonica, but there is a barrier that stops them from progressing in their soloing. The problem is that most players have their favorite licks, and when they have played them all, there's nothing else for them to play. At this point I'll challenge the player to take a 36 bar solo without playing the same lick twice. Usually they shrug their shoulders and say "36 Bars! How am I supposed to solo for 36 bars?" The soloing techniques that are taught in this section are designed to do just that. Every soloing musician's goal is to play every song with fresh new licks. Search in your mind to a group or performer that you have seen in person or listened to on a tape that every song sounded the same, I bet they lost your interest very quickly. After you finish studying this book I hope you're able to say with confidence "36 bars! How am I suppose fit all of my best licks into only 36 bars!"

Phrasing

To understand how phrasing works, it's as simple as listening to your own voice. When you make a statement or ask a question your voice pronunciation reflects it. For most people their voice rises in pitch when they ask a question and their voice lowers in pitch when they answer a question. By raising the pitch of your voice at the end of a statement you signal to the person you're talking to that you're expecting a response. By lowering the pitch of your voice at the end of a statement you signal to the person you're talking to that you've finished. In musical terms this is simply called question and answer. Listen to how the example below sets up this type of effect.

You can hear that the first half of the example asks a musical question that needs to be answered, with the second half of the example doing so. In the construction of music the I Chord and V Chord are the most structurally important chords in a piece. The V Chord, or fifth scale degree in our example, when set up properly sends the presentation of a place to rest away from the I Chord. The I Chord, or 1st scale degree, sends the clear presentation of being back or finished. When someone says that a solo was very melodic, their saying this because their ear picked up the phrasing that made the melody flow together well. As a soloist you're going to want to create this same type of phraseology to make your solos flow. As you start to develop this technique you'll find that you can set up the listener with a question and not answer it in the conventional way giving you some more time to solo before you finish. The example below asks a musical question and answers it, but right away a tail is thrown on telling the listener that you're not done yet.

How Phraseology Works Within A Solo

As you learn a new lick ask yourself how many bars does this lick take up, and what chord or chords does it work well above. By doing this, you start to build a mental vocabulary of licks that you can pull out any time during a solo. The first step is to review your one bar licks. One bar licks are usually to short to do conventional question and answer techniques, so they're used for filling the holes between a singer's verse and for background playing. The examples below shows some typical one bar licks.

The second step is to review your two bar licks. A two bar lick usually will have a one bar question and one bar answer. A two bar lick that lands on the I Chord is usually repeated the next two bars of the I Chord and will return after the IV Chord. A IV Chord lick that lasts for one bar can be repeated for the two other bars left over of the IV Chord. <u>This is the most used soloing technique to create unity within a 12 bar solo and to add length to an overall piece.</u> The example below shows a typical repeat scheme of a 12 bar solo.

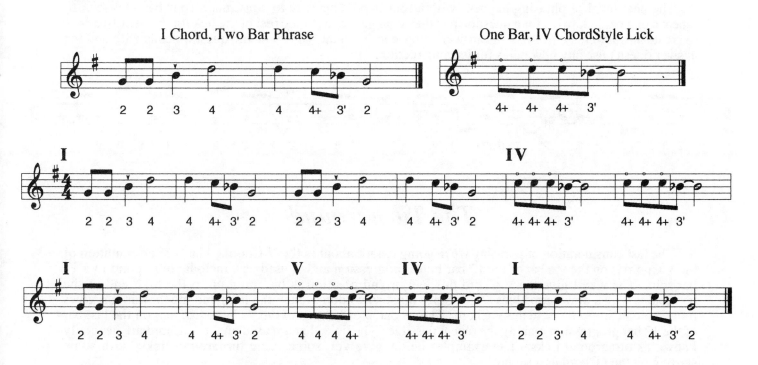

If you want to add variety in a two bar repeat, each time you come back to the original lick, change it either by changing the rhythmic feel or the notes themselves. The example below shows how the lick that was presented above can be changed to add variety in a solo.

63

The Four Bar Phrase

The next level of phrasing happens within four bars. One way to construct a four bar phrase is to repeat a one bar lick twice for a question and then change the rhythmic feel of the lick for the next two bars to create an answer. Notice that the answer below ends with the same note the question ends with and the answer doesn't use any new notes for its construction.

The Turnaround

The last consideration of phrasing we're going to talk about is the V Chord. The first presentation of the V Chord is on the 9th bar of the 12 bar blues progression and is used as a melodic high point in a 12 bar solo. The way I give the V Chord this feel in 2nd position is by going up to the high end of the harmonica with a draw harp blues scale. Since most solos don't touch the high end much, this run gives more melodic importance to the V Chord. The second presentation of the V Chord happens on the last bar of the 12 bar progression making the repeat possible. The licks that are used on the V Chord are generally known as turnaround licks. The examples below give you some basic turnaround licks, with some starting on the I Chord as a set up.

Octave Displacement

Octave displacement is the act of taking a note that would normally happen in one octave and displaces it into another octave. The concept is fairly simple, but octave displacement needs to be set up right to work effectively. The two main reasons I use octave displacement are to add contrast to my solo and to throw me into other ranges of my harmonica. The example below shows how you can jump up an octave to the high end to answer the musical question posed by the first lick.

2 3 4 5+ 6+ 5 4 4   2 3 4 5+ 9+ 9 8 9   8 6+

The question's run went up to 6 blow, which is G, and the answer repeated the same run, but instead of going to the expected 6 blow G, the lick went up an octave to the 9 blow G. What made this octave displacement successful was that I set up the listener to hear the 6 blow G, but went to the 9 blow G. What this octave displacement gave me was a way to go straight up to the high end without using a lengthy lick top get there. The example below shows how you can play around with octaves to give you a separated feel in your solo.

V   IV   I

1 2+ 2+ 1   4 4+ 4 4+   1+ 4+ 3' 4+ 3'   2

I have barely scratched the surface of what octave displacement is all about. If you would like to learn more about how you can get this type of effect in your solos listen to some jazz players. Jazz players use this effect way more extensively than blues players do.

Soloing Blocks

The technique of using soloing blocks is a way in which to get familiar with every part of your harmonica. An example would be to take a 36 bar solo only using the 1st, 2nd, and 3rd hole on your harmonica. The key to this exercise is your use of phrasing, if you just go off and jam with no plan in mind, within 6 bars your licks are going to sound very redundant. The 1st through 3rd hole, with bends, give you 12 notes to work with, but don't use them all at once. Introduce new notes as your solo progresses to give your playing a sense of building up to something. Below is a list of soloing blocks on the harmonica that you will find useful. For these exercises try some octave substitution, you'll find that it works very well.

Solo as long as you can using the:
1) 1st Through 3rd Hole Soloing Block
2) 2nd Through 4th Hole Soloing Block
3) 1st Through 4th Hole Soloing Block
4) 4th Through 6th Hole Soloing Block
5) 2nd Through 6th Hole Soloing Block
6) 6th Through 9th Hole Soloing Block
7) Combinations

Song Construction

When we talked about form in chapter 10, we only talked about the 12 bar blues format, but with well-written pieces there is a larger form at work. Vocal blues will usually follow an "AABA" format called rounded binary. The "A" section is a 12 bar verse that is repeated and the "B" section is a new verse that is followed by "A" to end. By adding the "B" section it adds a climax to a song that is otherwise redundant. As a soloist we can create this same type of effect using soloing blocks. To construct a song with this type of feel start off the solo with a 12 bar pattern that you think is really melodic and doesn't go all over the harmonica. This 12 bar solo is called the "head" and is going to open your song and close your song, so you want to make it really good. As you proceed through the rest of the song you're going to start on a low end block of your harmonica and then build up higher and higher as the song progresses in length. Finally at the end of the song repeat the head to signal to the listener that your finishing. Written below is a song outline that utilizes the soloing blocks to create this type of effect.

Example Song Outline

Do a 12 bar solo using:
    * Optional Introduction Solo
1) Head
2) 1st Through 3rd Hole Soloing Block
3) 1st Through 5th Hole Soloing Block
4) 1st Through 6th Hole Soloing Block
5) 1st Through 9th Hole Soloing Block (Song Climax)
6) Return To Head With An Ending Lick To Finish

Dynamics

You can play all the bluesy sounding licks you want in a solo, but without the use of dynamics your solos will lack the feeling and emotion blues is known for. Just as your voice can rise with intensity and emotion, so can your harmonica, making a mirror to your soul.

The Crescendo And Decrescendo / Cat & Mouse

The simplest usages of dynamics is the use of the crescendo and decrescendo. One way you can create this effect is instead of holding a note at one volume, increase the volume as the note gets longer, or decrease the volume as the note gets longer for a decrescendo. You can also use your hands for this effect by opening your cup to amplify the loud soft relationship. I like to accompany this effect with a delayed vibrato to add a more singing like quality to the effect. The cat and mouse effect is achieved by playing a lick at one volume and then decreasing the volume for the next lick like an echo. This effect is also achieved by playing a question lick at one volume and playing the answer at a softer volume.

Using Dynamics For Emotion

Written on the next page is a normal 12 bar progression. Before you listen to the tape play it yourself once to get a feel of the song, then play it a second time and add dynamics. After you have played, listen to the tape example and see if you came up with some of the same dynamic usage's. I hope that my example will give you a little bit of an idea of the scope available to you in using dynamics. Overall, even with all of these techniques, dynamics can't really be contained to words. Each usage is determined by what kind of emotion the performer is trying to portray. When you solo, challenge yourself to not just play licks, but use dynamics to add emotion. You'll find that you won't have to play a lot of licks to sound good, a couple slow licks played with a lot of emotion sounds just as good.

Using Dynamics In A Solo

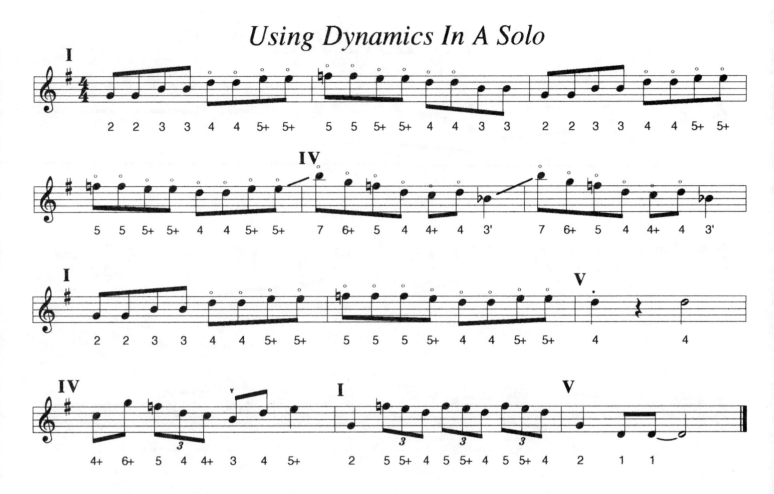

Using All The Soloing Techniques You've Learned

The song on pages 68 through 71 is an overall example of the lead techniques that you have learned in chapter 12. Looking at measure 1 through 4 notice that measures 3 and 4 are an octave substitution from measures 1 and 2. Challenge yourself to play all the high end notes in measures 3 and 4 tongue blocked, you'll find that you'll get a much thicker sound. Notice in measure 9 that I use a half step bend marking on the 5 draw. Keep in mind that there is no diatonic half step bend available on the 5 draw, there is only about an equivalent to a quarter tone bend available. The reason I have put a half step bend indicator is to keep the reading of the music easy; just keep in mind that it's a stylistic bend not a half step bend. Looking at the example song outline on page 66 as a reference, this first 12 bar solo is the introduction. The head is the second 12 bar solo that starts on measure 13, and comes back on measure 75 to end the song. Notice the strong phrasing that I use in this song; many of the solos are bases upon a basic repeat pattern shown on page 63. The third 12 bar solo, that starts on measure 25, utilizes the 1st hole through 3rd hole soloing block. The fourth 12 bar solo, that starts on measure 37, utilizes the 1st hole through 5th hole soloing block. In chapter 4 on two hole shakes I showed how you can take a melodic line and make a variation of it by taking the bottom notes and turning them into a shake. In the fourth 12 bar solo measure 37 and 38 is the original lick, and measure 41 and 42 is the variation. Notice that on the variation the bottom notes are exactly the same as the original lick. This is a great example of this technique. The fifth 12 bar solo, that starts on measure 49, utilizes the 1st hole through 6th hole soloing block. On measure 50 a "WA" indication is given. This notation tells you that you are to play each note using a WA sound from your hands; this WA effect is discussed in chapter 6. The sixth 12 bar solo, that starts on measure 61, utilizes the 1st hole through 9th hole soloing block, this 12 bar solo is the climax. On measure 61 a WA marking is indicated on the 2nd and 4th beat. The way this is meant to be played is to have your hands closed on the 1st and 3rd beat, and your hands open on the 2nd and 4th. This gives a rhythmic tone effect. Measure 69 is on the V Chord and I pretty much just use a straight forward draw harp blues scale, as you can hear, it makes for a nice effect. The last 12 bar solo starting on measure 73 is a repeat of the head with an ending style lick. Take your time on this song and have fun!

Big Boy's Jam

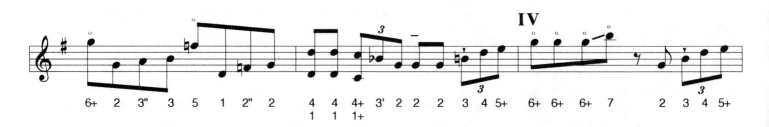

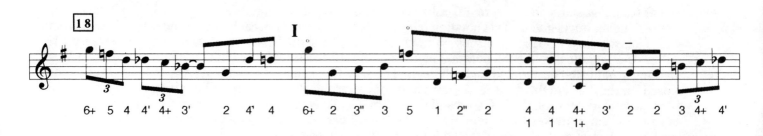

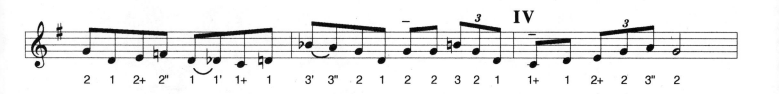

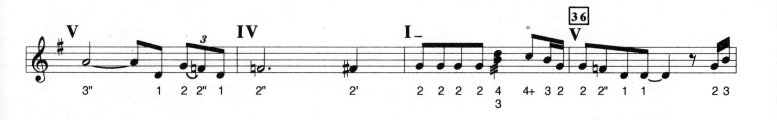

Soloing Techniques

Accompaniment Playing

When you solo, the other musicians respect you by backing you up and doing whatever they can to make you sound good. As a musician, when someone is singing or soloing it's your job to do what ever you can to make them sound good, even if it means not playing until it's your solo. Harmonica players have earned the notorious reputation for stepping on other musician's feet. Before you go up to perform, either with your band or as a guest artist, you need to ask yourself are you there to make the band sound great, or are you there to make yourself sound great. Then after you've finished, ask yourself if you accomplished what you set out to do. By asking yourself these simple questions before and after a performance you'll improve your outlook on the creation of music and if you play as a guest artist a lot I bet you'll be asked back to play more often. I feel the best way to learn how to play with a band is to learn what they're playing. Written below are some bass like progressions for the harmonica that can be used in the background. The examples are ordered from least protrusive to most protrusive; most protrusive being more soloistic than backup oriented.

Backup 12 Bar Progressions

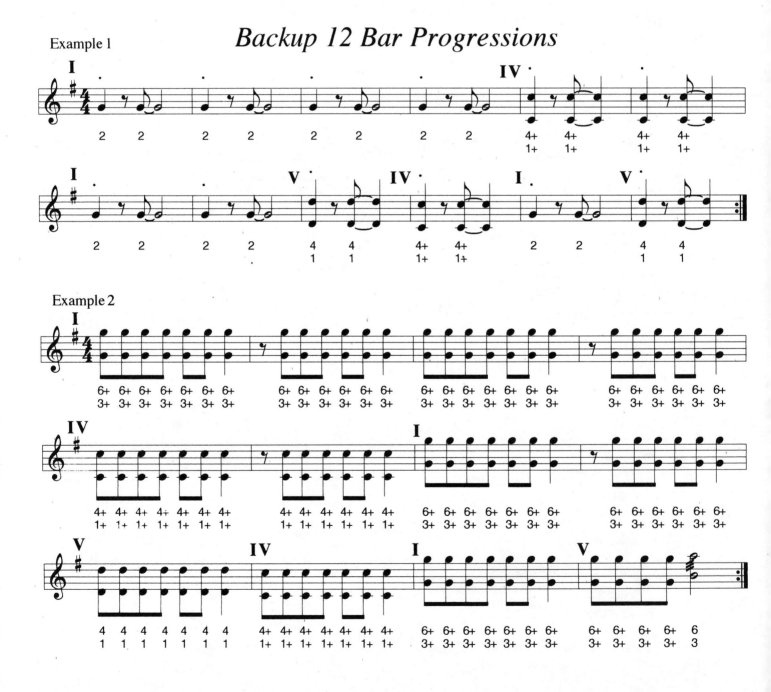

Example 1

Example 2

Example 3A: 2nd Position

Example 3B: 3rd Position

Example 4

Soloing Techniques

Example 5

74

As stated before in Chapter 10, the strongest musical agreement you can have with the accompaniment is to play root notes. Examples 1, 2, and 3 are all root oriented making your playing blend in more with the band rather than sticking out. When playing backup I'm a big user of root notes in octaves, like example 2. As stated in the chapter about tongue blocking, octaves send the presentation of one big note, thus thickening your tone like an organ. Examples 4 and 5 are the type of progressions that a bass player might play, and example 6 is the most soloistic of all the progressions. I use progressions like example 6 when a song reaches a climax, otherwise it's too protrusive.

Filling Holes

Most all well known harmonica players sing and play in the same song; because of this, the harmonica grew up as an instrument used for filling the holes between lyrics and solos. The normal blues verse is sung in two bar intervals, with the harmonica player playing on every other two bars. This means that when the harmonica player is filling the holes between lyrics he or she is actually playing up to 6 bars in a normal verse. Within these holes a harmonica player will play small licks that take up one to two bars that set up the next chord change. When the harmonica player isn't filling the holes he or she will either stop playing or play root notes to help fill out the sound of the band.

Listening To Other Musical Lines

As a soloist, you want to always keep your ears open to what the other musicians are playing. By doing this you can shape your licks to conform to the feel of the song and give yourself some great ideas to use in your solo. The easiest songs to solo with are ones with lyrics that have a strong discernible melody to follow. These types of songs just scream out copy me! By using the melody line as a basis for your solo you can mix little bits and pieces of the melody and your style together into an original solo that adds tremendously to the entirety of the song. If you catch on to a lick or phrase that is repeated in a song, you'll want to copy it the next time around. Most really good songs do have a catch phrase that sets them apart from other songs. By playing the catch phrase along with the other musicians it will help you fit in as a musical part in the song and sometimes the phrase in itself is enough to play as background until your time to solo.

When The Band Says They're Playing In Minor

When you're asked to play in a minor key with a band you're still going to play with the same harmonica that you would if the band were in major. If you stick to the blues scales while soloing you'll run into no problems soloing, technically you're playing more on the minor side anyway while soloing to blues. There are a couple of things I would like to talk to you about that you should keep in mind while soloing in a minor key. Written below is an example of the relationship between the minor scale and the blues scale.

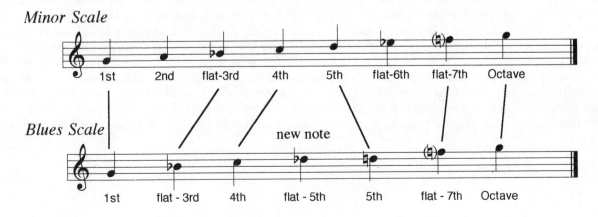

Soloing Techniques

The blues scale uses every note of the minor scale except the 2nd scale degree and the 6th scale degree. The second scale degree is fairly neutral, but the 6th isn't, the 6th scale degree alone sends the message of minor. In some positions on the harmonica the 6th scale degree isn't lowerable, making playing in a minor key somewhat tricky. In 2nd position the 2 blow and 5 blow are used often to give you a lighter feel in your solos, but the 2 blow and 5 blow aren't lowerable to make the flat-6 in the minor scale. You're going to want to stay away from these holes during a solo in minor because of the dissonance's created. Another hint about playing in minor is to play as many blue notes as you can. Since the blue notes themselves are more on the minor side than any other notes, you'll want to play them the most.

The Blues Break

Probably one of the most well known traits of blues is the use of the break. A break adds variety to a song that would otherwise just keep on repeating. Below shows some of the most common breaks used by harmonica players.

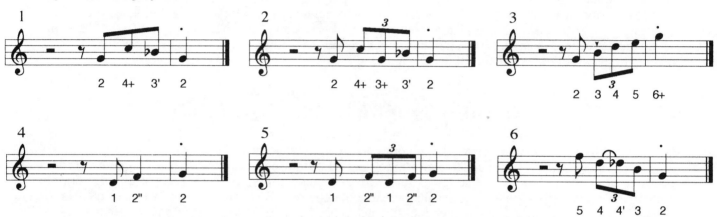

As you can see there are many different licks you can use for a break, in fact you can use almost any lick as long as it starts on the·upbeat of the 3rd beat, and ends on 'the downbeat of the next measure.

Extended Chord Usages

The toughest thing as a soloist you'll ever have to deal with is when a band plays chords that aren't within the traditional 12 bar progression. As people evolve so do their music, blues was the basis for Jazz and Rock & Roll. These musical styles evolved from someone who took blues to its limits, and then some. Even if a band calls itself a blues band, it doesn't mean that they're going to play all blues tunes. As a soloist you should be able to adapt to the different styles. As we studied the I, IV, and V Chord we found root notes and blues scales on those root notes to solo with. When given a new chord to work with the first thing you should do is listen to the chord and see if you can find any notes on your harmonica that match. If you can't find a note that matches, ask another musician in the band what the chord is. After you know the name of the chord, look at the note spread of your harmonica on the harmonica position chart that corresponds to the key you're using (pg. 56). After you have found your key, look at where all the root notes of that chord lands, the root notes will give you the best agreement with the band. After you've aquatinted yourself with the root notes look for the rest of the chord tones. By finding the chord tones in the chord you can solo around them just as you do with the blues scale chord tones. If you're unable to find any notes of the chord on your harmonica you might think about changing to a position that does have the notes. Overall, extended chords don't happen much in blues, but if they do they usually only last for one measure and playing a root note like you would on the V Chord in 2nd position works just fine.

~Applying What You've Learned~

What I would like to accomplish in this chapter is to tie up some loose ends, summarize key points, and give you some final insight into the fine art of being a musician. Since this book is mostly of techniques and concepts I would strongly recommend going through it twice. There will be many things that you'll catch on to the second time around that you either didn't get at all or just didn't sink in the first read through.

Tone

One of the toughest questions to answer posed by a harmonica student is "How can I get the sweet fat tone you have?" My stock answer is time and practice, but there are some very viable techniques that you can use that will help you to get the tone you desire. Point One: Don't settle for second best! If you like a technique or a tone created by a certain procedure, don't cut your self short . . . learn it! Most everything good on God's green earth takes time and perseverance. Point Two: Do your single holes sing? The most basic aspect of your tone relies on how cleanly you can play a single hole. If your single hole sounds pinched, either your lips are too tight, or your tongue is in a place where it is constricting your natural airflow. To stop your lips from pinching, play with an overall wider embouchure and you might find that tilting the harmonica helps in getting a clearer tone. If that doesn't change your sound, it's probably your tongue. When bending a note on the harmonica a constricted air passage must be created. If your tone sounds either bent or pinched, it's a possibility that your tongue is in a place where it is creating a constricted air flow. Try moving your tongue up higher or lower in your mouth and as your playing pronounce a syllable that makes your entire mouth larger. Try some of these syllables and see if they help your sound: AW, O, I, or T. Point Three: Think of all the techniques that you can use to fatten your sound. I always say to my students that we play a small tinny sounding instrument and what ever we can do to make the harmonica sound otherwise, do it! The use of the throat vibrato is one of the best techniques you can use to help your tone. The vibrato takes off all the rough edges and gives your playing a more singing like quality. The use of the tongue slap and octaves are also very strong factors in fattening your sound. Remember that the largest reason for using octaves is to send a broader message of one note. I guarantee if you use tongue blocking your tone will improve. Point Four: Experiment. When I learn a new lick I'll try to rearrange it until it's exactly the way I want it to sound. Point Five: Use your cupping techniques to their fullest. When playing acoustically, keep in mind all the tone effects you can create just from opening and closing your hands. When playing with a bullet microphone my best advice is to make sure that at all times you have that one finger's distance between the face of the microphone and your harmonica. It's also very important that your cupping is airtight.

Playing Bluesy Vs. Playing Light

If you want to sound bluesy, play within the blues scale. If you want to have a lighter feel to your playing, don't play within the blues scale. It's as simple as that! To play bluesy, you want to make use of the blue notes at every possible opportunity. These blue notes are what depict the minor side verses the major side. For a lighter feel in your playing your going to want to avoid these blue notes by playing the blue notes that are usually bent, natural. Written below is the major scale on your harmonica in 2nd position. As you play though this scale notice that the 7th scale degree should be raised, but isn't available to us. After you play this scale compare the major scale and the blues scale on the next page.

	2	3"	3	4+	4	5+	5	6+
Scale Degrees —	1st	2nd	3rd	4th	5th	6th	7th	Octave

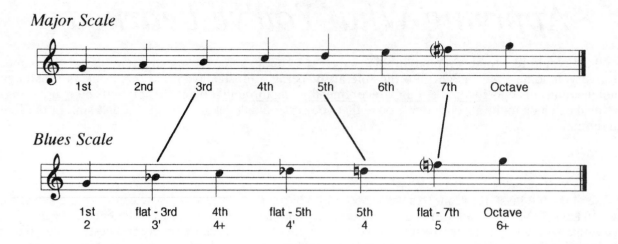

Major Scale

1st 2nd 3rd 4th 5th 6th 7th Octave

Blues Scale

1st	flat - 3rd	4th	flat - 5th	5th	flat - 7th	Octave
2	3'	4+	4'	4	5	6+

Notice that the blues scale gets rid of the 2nd (3") and 6th (5+) scale degrees and lowers the 3rd (3'). Take notice that the 7th scale degree (5) should be sharped, but isn't available. Whenever playing the 5 draw you are playing a blue note, so if you want to play with a lighter feel avoid the 5 draw by substituting it with the 5 blow.

To Get A Lighter Feel In Your 2nd Position Soloing

Substitute 5 draw with 5 blow. Substitute 2 draw whole step bend with 2 blow. Use the 3 draw, whole step bend more often. Always play the 3 draw unbent. Avoid the use of blue notes and the 2/5, 3/6 draw octaves.

To Get A Bluesier Feel In <u>All</u> Your Soloing

Make the majority of the notes in your solo from the blues scale. Extensively use blue notes. Written below is an example of how you can drastically change the sound of a lick by the use of these rules.

Light

2 3 4 4+ 3 4+ 3 2

Bluesy

2 3' 4' 4+ 3' 4+ 3' 2

In Closing

I hope that this book gave you some excitingly new insight into what your harmonica is truly capable of doing. These concepts that I have developed haven't only improved my students technical capabilities on the harmonica, but my own as well. Unlike many physical techniques on the harmonica, these are techniques of the brain that grow stronger the more you use them. My goal in writing this book was to make it the most comprehensive book ever written for the advanced harmonica student. I hope that I have lived up to my expectations. Take these techniques and use them to their fullest potential and I guarantee you will come out a better player for it. Thanks for your ear, and good luck!

~Glossary Of Terms~

Accent: A marking that adds emphasis on one note or chord.

Arpeggiated: The notes of a chord played one after another instead of all at the same time.

Bar Lines: Lines that dissect the staff into measures.

Beam: A line used to connect consecutive eighth notes instead of having all the eighth note with individual flags.

Beat: The segmentation of time into a pulse. **ex.** When taping your foot you are creating a pulse or beat; in 4/4 time there are four beats.

Bend: The actual act of the bend is achieved by the interaction of your tongue and roof of your mouth to create a constricted air passage that bends the pitch of the note that corresponds to the hole in which you are playing.

Chord: A vertical structure created when three or more notes in thirds are struck simultaneously (all at the same time), or arpeggiated (one right after the other).

Diatonic: The word diatonic, when associated with a scale, means that there are five whole steps and two half steps that it uses for its construction.

Dissonant: A word used to describe something that isn't pleasant to the ear. When two notes are sounded that are only a half step or a hole step apart they considered to sound dissonant.

Duration: The amount of prescribed time that a note is to be held.

Flat: A sign that is notated in front of a note head that means that you are to perform that note one half step lower than normally played. To say that an instrument sounds flat, is stating that in comparison to the other instruments, that particular instrument has a slightly lower pitch than the others, thus making that instrument sound dissonant.

Hemiola: A ratio of three in the time that there normally would be two (3:2).

Home Base: A word used to describe the tonic or central pitch in a song. The key in which a song is played.

Key: A system of notes that are used in the construction of a song

Lick: A small piece of music that can be used to contribute to a whole.

Major Scale: A diatonic scale where the half steps happen between the third and fourth scale degrees, and between the seventh scale degree and octave. **ex.** If you were to play all the white keys on the piano from C to C you would get a major scale.

Measure: The distance of time between two bar lines. Sometimes the measure is called a bar, both these terms in that context are synonymous. **ex.** In 4/4 time, a measure would be four beats.

Melodic: A word used to say that a musical line uses mostly notes that are within the scale you are working within. When you say that some one's playing sounds melodic, you are stating that it flows well within the key.

Melody: The musical line within a piece that is most active. The melody is also sometimes called the tune.

Minor Scale: A diatonic scale where the half steps happen between the second and third scale degree, and between the fifth and sixth scale degree. **ex.** If you were to play all the white keys on the piano from A to A you would get a minor scale.

Note Head: The round part of the note that where it rests on the staff determines what pitch that note is.

Pitch: Any sound, high or low, that can be determined to have musical characteristics

Riff: A small piece of music that can be used to contribute to a whole.

Scale: A system of notes that run from one note to its octave.

Sharp: A sign that is notated in front of a note head that means that you are to perform that note one half step higher than normally played. To say that an instrument sounds sharp is stating that in comparison to the other instruments, that particular instrument has a slightly higher pitch than the others, thus making that instrument sound dissonant.

Simultaneously: At the same time.

Staccato: A marking that is used when a note or chord is to be played with a short attack and duration.

Staff: A system of horizontal lines, on and between which, notes are written to indicate pitch.

Standard Notation: A music notational system that is universally used by musicians.

Thanks To . . .

All the musicians from the past and present that make harmonica what it is today.

Mel Bay for believing in this book.

My students, for without them there would be no book.

God for music, and my parents for helping me develop it.

Photography By: Dave Lapori, 385 North Third Street A-3, San Jose, CA 95112

Comments Regarding This Book Can Be Sent To Me, David Barrett At:

David Barrett's "Building Harmonica Technique"
P.O. Box 1723
Morgan Hill, CA 95038